Jack Grout's
GOLF CLINIC

Jack Nicklaus' Teacher and Coach

Introduction by Jack Nicklaus

The Athletic Institute
North Palm Beach, Florida

We acknowledge the contribution of the historical photos by the PGA of America and the World Golf Hall of Fame.

Printed in the United States of America
0 9 8 7 6 5 4 3 2

To my wife Bonnie,
mother of our four children

Introduction

Watch good golfers and you'll notice that they all seem to swing the club a little differently. Really study them, however, and you'll see that they also do certain things similarly — even identically. A prime example is the head: it rarely moves more than fractionally from the beginning of the swing until well past impact with the ball.

Those commonalities of the good players are the basic fundamentals of golf technique. They really haven't changed much in an awful long time, and there aren't a whole lot of them. But they have to be understood and mastered if you are to play the game **consistently** *at or close to the maximum of your potential.*

The sooner a budding golfer learns these fundamentals, the quicker he'll build a solid swing, and the longer it will last. And that's where I was so fortunate as a kid back in Columbus, Ohio, in 1950. Just as my dad was getting me interested in golf, Jack Grout arrived as the new professional at Scioto Country Club and began a weekly class for juniors. I joined, then quickly persuaded Dad to let me take additional private lessons from the new pro. Those sessions were the beginning of the most productive and enjoyable relationship I've ever had in golf.

It was productive first because Jack Grout had the knowledge and ability and enthusiasm to teach me the true fundamentals of the golf swing before I could groove and then have to unlearn bad habits. Under his direction and motivation, I was able to start correctly and continue correctly, which saved me untold time and energy in building a solid game.

It was productive also because, by having the patience to stick to simple basics in answering my hundreds of questions, Jack gave me a sound mental comprehension of what I was trying to do with a golf club, to the point where I could eventually correct or "teach" myself without having to run back to him every time I hit a bad shot. And, as Bobby Jones said, if there's a secret to playing really good golf over a fair spell of time, the ability to self-correct unquestionably is it.

Finally, it was productive because over all the years since first starting golf I've had a friend and teacher who knows me and my game intimately to fall back on whenever I've experienced a problem beyond self-solution, as every golfer will do from time to time. Jack made all of this even easier, because a nicer man there never was.

What you'll learn in this book is what Jack Grout first taught me back at Scioto in 1950, and what he's been instilling in me one way or another ever since. Pay close attention and, with just a little patience, you might really surprise yourself out there on the golf course.

You've got a great teacher. If you can be just half as good a pupil, I'm certain you'll find this game a whole lot easier and more enjoyable.

And, once again, Jack, thanks a million, not only for all that help over all that time, but for being such a fabulous friend.

— Jack Nicklaus

JACK GROUT: *"I learned golf as a child in Oklahoma City and have been in love with it ever since."*

Foreword

This new golf instruction book might be called a sequel to my earlier publication, ON THE LESSON TEE, in the language of editors and publishers. In the language of a golf teacher, it is more like a follow-through.

The first book was a lesson, as the title said, that dealt with the basic golf fundamentals. It was designed to make the reader's introduction to golf as uncomplicated as possible and to give him an eager and rewarding send-off in our game.

Now we step into JACK GROUT'S GOLF CLINIC, and the difference will be about the same as between a lesson and a clinic. We will be getting more detailed as we talk about the mechanics of the golf swing, the planning of specific shots, and some of the technical aspects of playing equipment. This book will appeal particularly to anyone who has been around golf long enough to be fascinated with the more intricate aspects of the golf swing — their own golf swing.

Most of the great players I have known, and especially Jack Nicklaus, can take their own golf swings apart like a fine watch. They can find the flaws, eliminate them, and reconstruct their swings. But even the great players seldom take on this job alone. They go to their personal professionals or instructors almost as regularly as most people go to a barber or hair dresser. The average golfer, on the other hand , probably cannot visit his instructor quite that frequently. But when he does, it is important that he understands the diagnosis and corrections the teacher is imparting.

While the wise doctor will not treat himself, it is altogether likely he will be able to spot his own symptoms because of his vast knowledge of how the human body functions. It stands to reason, then, that the reader who understands the many elements of the golf swing and how they fit together will benefit more from lessons and practice.

Now and then I am sure some of this instruction will appear a little confusing. Those of us who teach golf know how intricate the golf swing can be as it relates to muscle memory and behavior, along with many other considerations, including human limitations, attitudes and even psychological factors. But don't be discouraged. If you reach a feeling of being overwhelmed, just put the book down and pick up a golf club. Do a little swinging or, if it is convenient, spend a little time on a practice range. Then come back to the book and re-read the section. Chances are it will have cleared up magically for you.

Please understand this is not a book to be read rapidly by someone expecting to shave a lot of strokes off his game immediately. If golf instruction worked like that, all of us who teach would seem like magicians. This might be regarded more like a reference book to which the serious player or student of the golf swing might go for advanced learning. When he feels his swing slipping, he will be better able to trace the problem; or when his instructor finds a flaw, they will be able to talk about it in the same language.

We will be getting into specifics very early in this book and you won't be very far along until we are talking about ankle roll and wrist cock and ball flight patterns. If these and other terms are not clear to you now, I feel sure they will be by the time you have been through JACK GROUT'S GOLF CLINIC.

It is my great pleasure to be able to bring these detailed chapters to you. I hope this book will find a prominent place in your golf library.

Even more important, I hope it will continue to occupy a prominent place in your golf game, a place you will go when you want to learn more about what makes a good golf swing a thing of beauty and a joy forever.

— Jack Grout

Contents

CHAPTER ONE

Selecting Your "Instruments"

———————

There's a well known fact among professional golfers who do a lot of teaching: you can't make up for lack of fundamentals with equipment. But it's also pretty hard to have correct fundamentals with equipment so ill-suited to you that you're fighting it with every swing!

The evolution of this game has affected every area and equipment is no exception. Today's golf clubs are researched, tried and tested a million different ways before they get to the marketplace. And with the standardization and quality controls available it is possible to get a good set of clubs in almost any price range.

For most golfers the costs of having a set of clubs made especially for them are prohibitive. But it is possible to have that done by going to one of the companies that specialize in making a specific set of clubs to meet the specific needs of an individual. Luckily, most golfers can find clubs that meet the majority of their specific needs right in the golf shop of their own courses. Let's look at a few things you should consider when you go club shopping.

If you can just remember that golf is not only a science, but is also an art, then you can understand why most people select golf clubs on how they look and how they feel. And this should not be underestimated as a factor. If you feel good about your clubs, you're likely to swing with more confidence and authority. And *both* of those things are necessary in making a good golf swing.

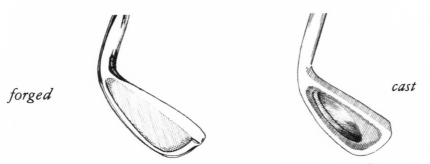

forged *cast*

IN BUYING CLUBS, *a choice must be made between forged or cast irons.*

But there are some other considerations to keep in mind. If you are buying irons, you should decide if you want *forged* or *cast* irons. Basically the difference is this: forged clubs are pounded or forged out of a piece of metal. Because each one is made separately, each one can be a shade different. Many well-skilled golfers, including most professionals, like the feel of a ball hitting the forged clubs. A cast club is one that has been poured or cast in a mold. Because the hot metal is poured into this mold, some variations can be made that can assist the golfer. For example, you will see some cast clubs that have a hollowed out back which creates more weight on the sole and the toe of the club. This helps many golfers get the ball airborne as well as to hit it straighter when the ball is struck off center on the club face. But the fact is both forged and cast clubs are good. Your choice should be the one you hit best with and most consistently. Chances are that will also be the one that has the best "feel" when you swing it and make contact.

The choice in wood clubs will be among three different substances: persimmon, laminated wood, and metal woods. Persimmon usually is the most expensive in most cases. The wood is carved from a block of persimmon, which is generally accepted to be the hardest, yet lightest, wood for golf clubs. Laminated clubs are made by laminating sheets of wood together to make a hard but light wood block from which the club is carved. And of course metal woods are those that have been cast in metal, often filled with a substance to give them the correct feel. Each of these materials makes excellent golf clubs. The wooden clubs, particularly the persimmon, is subject to damage from intense heat, such as your car trunk and/or from being kept wet, like in a head cover after playing on wet grass.

It should be mentioned here that some club manufacturers are offering a new type of "wood" clubhead made of graphite. Whether this becomes a really viable alternative for golfers or is just another cosmetic experiment remains to be seen at this writing.

In both woods and irons there are some general considerations that are present in all clubs. A standard set of clubs for either men or women meets the specifications for the average person. All clubs have a *length*. For most standard men's clubs the driver is about 43'' long, depending upon the manufacturer. A standard women's driver is around 42'' long. For men a 5-iron is about 37'' or 37½'' and for women, 35½'' or 36''. My feeling on the length of a club is a little different from some other professionals. I think that if you are not so tall and you have sound fundamentals, then you should have a club that's a little *longer* than standard! By having a club ½'' or 1'' longer you may be able to get more distance in your shots. Bobby Cruickshank, who was a successful professional back in the '30s, was only about 5'2'' and his driver was 46'' long. On the other hand if you're tall, playing with a shorter club gives you more control. With the amount of leverage a tall person has distance isn't so much of a problem. But before you run out and change the length of your clubs remember that changing the length of a club's shaft also changes its *lie*.

The lie of any club is an important consideration. It may seem confusing, but actually lie is nothing more than a measure of the angle between the ground and the back of the club shaft when the club is properly soled. Whereas length is primarily a measure of the distance from your knuckles to the ground when you stand upright, the correctness of your

3

BOBBY CRUICKSHANK *was a short golfer who used a longer-than-average driver.*

club's lie is determined by how you set up or address the ball. If you address the ball with your hands very low, you will need a flatter lie to your club than the person who stands more upright, all other things equal. So if your fundamental set-up is not sound even a club that has the correct lie for you will not be soled properly. If the lie of a club is too flat for you, the club will sit up on the toe at address; if it's too upright, the club will sit up on the heel with the toe in the air. Either one of these things can influence your golf shot. A correct lie will give you a swing in which the entire sole will strike the ground, not heel first or not toe first. Of course, that's again assuming you, the person holding on to the club, has made a good swing to start with! Remember? Fundamentals.

The shafts of clubs may have different degrees of flexibility. A standard men's set has "R" or regular flexibility and a standard ladies' set has "L" or sometimes "A" shafts. A general rule of thumb for you is that if your normal swing speed is fast and you are fairly strong, you can use a little stiffer shaft. The designation for these shafts, of course, is "S." But if you are not swinging as hard as you used to or if you rely on that smooth buggy-whip swing to get the job done, a shaft with more flexibility will be better for you.

It seems to me about the only thing most golfers know to talk about when discussing clubs is swingweight. While certainly an important ratio, it is far from the most important thing in selecting clubs. You need to consider swingweight, but you need to think about overall weight, too. It's pretty nearly impossible to create a lot of clubhead speed in your swing if the club's so heavy that it weighs you down, or that you get tired by the end of a round. But, by the same token, some of the ultra-light clubs now on the market don't give the golfer any feel for the clubhead. For the player used to swinging a more conventional club it feels like swinging a yardstick! A lighter weight club can add distance if you can add clubhead speed with it. But it's got to be heavy enough to pack a wallop.

CHAPTER ONE

I've seen a lot of ladies on my lesson tee and there are two problems I see frequently. One is that sometimes a ladies' club is so light that a strong woman doesn't get maximum distance from it. Or, on the other extreme, I see ladies who have had one of their husband's sets of clubs cut down shorter, and therefore made ever heavier, and she can't control it. You've got to have a club that feels good and that you can swing without losing control and that is a combination of both swingweight and static or overall weight.

I've saved one aspect of club components until last because it is the one link we have with that golf club . . . the grip. Grips on golf clubs come in all sorts of materials. Some players say that they really like the feel of leather; most people have some type of rubber composition because they are easier to care for than leather. But *so many* people DON'T care for their grips at all! To make a good swing, one with a good feeling and one that you can try to repeat, you need a grip that fits and a grip that helps you hang on to the club. You can check your grip for fitting just by holding the club in your left hand and seeing where your fingertips come. If they nearly touch your palm but are no more than ¼'' away from it, your grip fits. If your nails dig into your palms or there's a big space between your fingertips and the palm, you'd better have a professional look at your grips. Sizes of grips can be modified very easily by a qualified club repairer. A grip that fits will not only feel better but it will allow you to swing the club in a more controlled manner. A grip that's too big for you will contribute to your hitting that ball out to the right, and one that's too small will make it awfully easy for you to snap hook it off to the left.

In addition to a grip that fits, you should have a grip that has some tackiness. Most golfers never clean their grips, much less replace them. Feel your club's grips. Are they slick and slippery? That makes it very hard to hang onto during the swing. An old toothbrush is useful in cleaning

6

grips. Shampoo or dish detergent will remove the body oil and perspiration from your hands that builds up on grips. But if you have leather grips, don't use the toothbrush. Use some saddle soap or leather cleaner. And for most golfers the grips should be replaced every year or two. They get too hard and slick. Do yourself a favor and keep your contact point with the golf club in good shape.

The bottom line for any golfer goes right back to fundamentals. If you have equipment that is right for you, that has a good feel, and that is in good repair, you have the tools you need. Many golfers today are using the clubs they've had for years. They just have them repaired, refinished and regripped and they're as good as new.

Even professional golfers hang onto favorite clubs. I remember an experience from my days playing the Tour. I was working for Henry Picard up in Hershey, Pa., and he and I were traveling the Tour together during the season. Henry had been playing some pretty fancy golf himself that had earned him the nickname of the ''Hershey Hurricane.'' He had been the leading money winner on the winter tour in 1935, the same year he set a new single round scoring record at the Masters with a first round 68. He led the event for two days but then had a bad front nine on that soggy Saturday that saw Gene Sarazen hole out his four wood on the 15th hole for the famous double-eagle. Even though Picard finished only fourth in the 1935 Masters, he went on to win it in 1938. And, in my estimation, he was the top player in America in those years between 1936 or '37 and 1940.

On this particular day in 1937, I remember we were at a Tour stop in San Francisco. Sam Snead, who was also in his heyday around this time, was playing the event, too. Sam was having an awful time hitting his drives. He couldn't play any club he had or find any club he liked. We were watching him fight it out on the practice tee when Henry said, ''Hey Sam, I got a driver I think you'd like.''

HENRY PICARD, *"the Hershey Hurricane,"* was both a player and a clubmaker.

"Where is it?"

"In my car."

"Where's your car?"

"Right over there."

"Well get it out!"

Snead swung the club with that great rhythm of his and ripped it down the middle. Then again and again.

"How much?" he asked.

"Five dollars," was the reply. Now, there was nothing fancy about this club. It was a club Henry had made, a double-out driver, stained brown with a good shaft and a leather grip. Sam Snead paid Henry Picard $5 for it in 1937 and then played with it constantly through the '60s! He had it refinished. He had it refaced. He had the sole plate put back on even after it started falling out from rot and age. And he kept using it!

It only goes to show you, once you find a club or a set of clubs you like and one that fits you and your swing, you should stick with it. Just like there are no gimmicks in the swing, there are no magic clubs. Some clubs are better suited for your size, your strength and your game than others. Find them and stick with them. Then work to make your swing fundamentals better.

I remember the young Ben Hogan just learning the game in Texas. He was a teenager playing at the Glen Garden Club where my brother was a professional and I would also make a few dollars teaching with him there. Ben had seven clubs then. And not only were they not a matched set . . . three were left-handed and four were right-handed clubs! Well, Ben would hook when he hit left-handed and hook when he hit right-handed so he couldn't decide which way to play. My brother gave him three more hickory-shafted, right-handed clubs and we persuaded him to play right-handed. He then went to work on his fundamentals and his technique, just like you will be doing. And as we all know the rest is history.

BEN HOGAN *developed into one of the best strikers of the golf ball.*

He became one of the best strikers of the golf ball ever to play.

In the same way that you need professional guidance and coaching in developing sound swing techniques, you will need professional guidance in selecting the best clubs for yourself. A PGA or LPGA professional can be of the greatest assistance in finding that special group of instruments for you. Most of these professionally trained individuals will be happy to evaluate your present equipment and make suggestions for repairs and / or replacements if necessary.

If you are going to try to learn a correct movement pattern, you will want to practice it with the correct implements. Once you have them, it's time for the work to begin.

CHAPTER TWO

Using, Not Losing Your Head in Golf

One of the questions that I am asked most often as Jack Nicklaus's teacher is, "What is the one thing Nicklaus does best in this game?" My answer is always the same. He uses his brain! There's no doubt that there are some techniques of which he is truly a master. But the thing I think that sets him apart and has contributed to his winning so many different titles is how much he knows and how well he thinks around the golf course.

In order to make yourself a better player you will have to master some of this same knowledge just as Jack Nicklaus has. Unless you understand the basic laws of physics that control a round ball being hit by an implement, and unless you understand what you will be trying to do with your fundamental skills, you will not be able to make progress in your playing skills.

And not only will you need to understand these basic theories and fundamentals, you will also need to know how to use your mind out on the golf course. You will need to know how to control your emotions. And you will need to know how to analyze each playing situation in which you find yourself. This may sound like more conscious effort than you really want to devote to a game, but let me assure you, when these factors become natural and automatic, you'll not only enjoy golf more, but you will feel a genuine sense of personal accomplishment.

For the moment let's get your mind working to understand the basic laws that govern what happens when club meets ball. By understanding

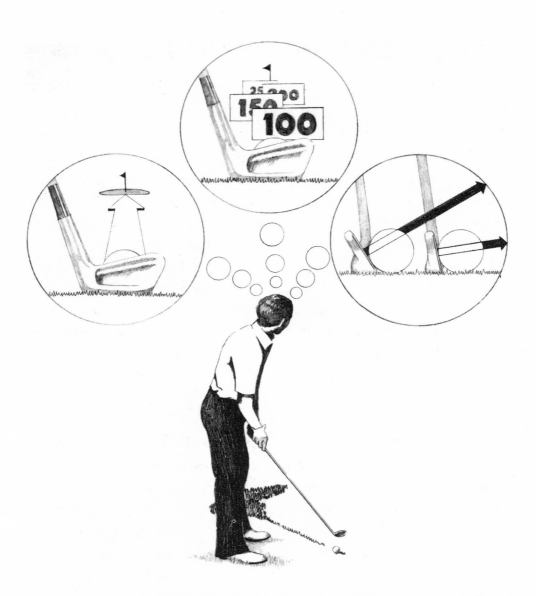

REMEMBER *the three basic properties of the golf shot.*

these laws and theories you can better evaluate your own abilities. And you can become a more discriminating learner yourself because you will be better equipped to evaluate what you read, see or hear about the golf swing.

Every shot you hit in golf will have three different properties: direction, distance, and trajectory or height. The exception to this statement is putting, having no *intended* trajectory. There is the story however about the amateur, who had not been playing well at all in the Bing Crosby Pro-Am at Pebble Beach. Somewhere around the seventeenth or maybe even

"DUTCH" HARRISON *played the game during the first half of this century.*

15

the eighteenth hole he had the chance to make a long putt for the team's best score on that hole. He nervously asked his professional partner, Dutch Harrison, what his best strategy was. Harrison's reply was, "Try to keep it low!"

One or more of these ball flight properties will be influenced by each of these physical laws. And while I certainly don't expect you to think about them with every shot, knowing them allows you to understand every shot you hit.

CLUBHEAD SPEED

Everything else being equal in your swing, the faster the clubhead is moving, the longer your shot will be. There are two things that are very important in that statement: (1) "everything else being equal" implies that there are a number of other things in the swing that can be less efficient and therefore causing you a loss of distance; (2) the "faster the *clubhead* is moving" means that you will want to work on fundamentals that contribute to making the clubhead go faster, not the whole swing go faster, particularly at the wrong times during the swing. If your swing is fundamentally sound, then clubhead speed is the single *greatest* determinant of distance.

SWING PATH

As many of you know, distance, while good for the ego, may not be good for the golf score unless it is combined with direction. One of the greatest influences on where your golf ball will go is the actual path or direction you swing along. When you swing your club directly along your target line at impact, your ball will fly directly out toward your target . . . at least in the *beginning* of the shot. Whether it stays on that line or eventually spins off to one side or another is an additional concept we will address in just one moment. But if you swing your club across that target line, the ball will follow that path you're swinging along in its initial flight. An inside to outside swing path will cause a right-handed golfer to start the ball out to the right. An outside-inside swing path will cause a right-handed golfer to start the ball out to the left. Whether or not that ball remains on that line depends upon any sidespin on the ball.

An important consideration for you to know is that your swing's path is predominantly determined by the position of your shoulders at impact. If your shoulders are facing your target line at impact, that is, the shoulder line running parallel to the target line, the ball will start out toward the target. Conversely, if the shoulder line is left of the target or right of the target the ball will start out left or right of the target, respectively.

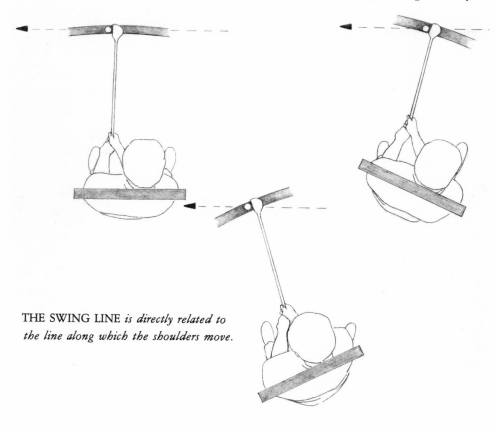

THE SWING LINE *is directly related to the line along which the shoulders move.*

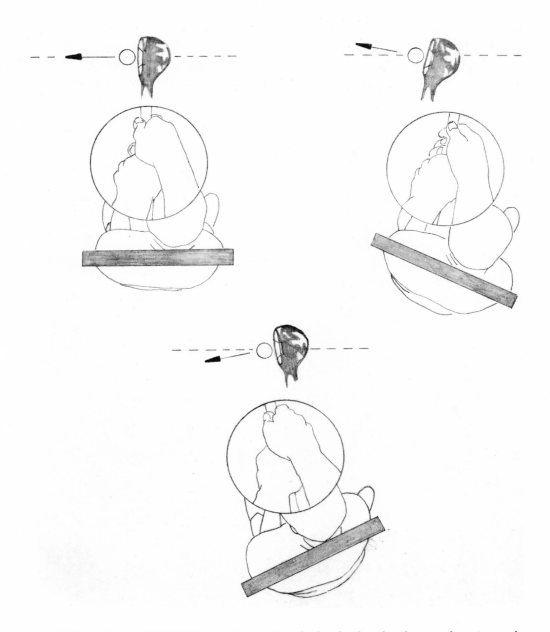

THE CLUB FACE POSITION, *determined by the hands, directly relates to the swing path.*

CLUBFACE POSITION

The other major determinant of direction in a golf shot is the position of the clubface at the moment of impact with the ball. Actually it can only be in one of three positions: square, open or closed. The thing that a lot of golfers don't understand is "square, open or closed" to WHAT?

A simple explanation is this: the clubface position is determined by the position of the hands at impact. Because the hands are connected by the arms to the shoulders, then the clubface is always square, open or closed to the SWING PATH. Now think about that one for a minute. Yes, the clubface can be square, open or closed to the target line, but the effect of the clubface position on the ball relates only to how it is lined up (or not lined up) squarely with the swing path.

Now can you see what will happen if you make a bad swing where your upper body and shoulders rush the downswing and therefore come outside the line before impact BUT the hands are still facing the target line? The results will be a ball that starts to the left because the swing path is outside-inside but ends up curving (or) slicing back toward the center because the hands kept the clubface open to the actual swing line. And in this case, you would need to work not on faster hand action to close the clubface but on more efficient upper body action to keep the shoulders parallel to the target line at impact rather than across it at impact. Faster hand action would result in your clubface becoming square with your swing path and the shot results would be a pull to the left of target.

Knowing that a clubface position that is square keeps the ball flying along the original path of the swing, a position that is open causes the ball to slice away from you, and a position that is closed causes the ball to hook back toward you is something you absolutely have to understand. Otherwise you have no way to understand what is making your ball be hooked, sliced, pushed, pulled, or even how you hit it straight.

When you do not have the clubface square to the swing path it affects another aspect of your shot. A clubface that is not square hits the ball with a glancing blow. The fact that a glancing blow is not as forceful as a square blow means that the total distance of your shot is affected by clubface position also. An open clubface creates a weaker hit than a square or closed clubface. This means that a slice might be significantly shorter than either a straight shot or a hooked shot. And the type of spin imparted by a closed clubface gives additional roll to the ball after it hits the ground. If the shot has curved significantly that roll will only put you further into trouble. If you have planned your shot well it will add playable distance!

Before going on to the two remaining physical laws I want you to stop for a minute and consider how these last two are ultimately intertwined. Seldom if ever do even the touring pros hit the ball absolutely straight. Everyone has tendencies, if not outright techniques, that contribute to some type of curve in their shots. The secret is to determine which is your tendency, to play the ball from right to left or to play the ball from left to right. Bobby Jones was predominantly a right to left player. Most of the pros who used a more classical type of golf swing and who wanted to take advantage of the additional roll of a hooking, or at least a drawing ball preferred to play it right to left. Ben Hogan, once he got rid of those youthful "death-hooks" went on to become primarily a left to right player. Jack Nicklaus has primarily been a left to right player. And a number of today's young strong professionals who hit the ball such a long distance that they do not need additional roll like to hit the ball high and with what has been called the "tour fade." This shot, while effective in stopping the ball on an approach shot often works against the average amateur player who plays a severe slice developed from a poor swing pattern rather than a delicate well-controlled tour fade!

To play all the shots necessary in golf you have to learn to control both the swing path and the clubface position. Once having learned that, you can control your ball flight direction to play under any and all conditions.

ANGLE OF ATTACK

While there is a minimum amount of influence on ball flight trajectory by clubface position (an open clubface produces a higher flight than does a square clubface and a closed clubface produces a lower ball flight

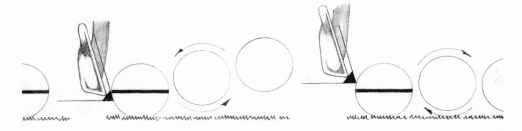

A BALL THAT IS WELL-STRUCK
must be hit below the equator, that imaginary line around its center.

than either of the other two), the angle at which the club is swung down into the ball is the primary determinant of trajectory. Complementing that is the idea of exactly where the club hits the ball.

Before you get worried that this is going to become a total physics lecture, think of it this way: The ball, like any round object has an equator . . . an imaginary line around its center. To get the ball airborne you have to hit it below that equator with a lofted club. It is as simple as that. When you "scull" it, you have simply hit the ball above the center.

The angle at which your club approaches or attacks the ball is determined by two things: (1) what club you are using and (2) how vertically you swing the club down behind the ball. You can readily see that a driver does not have a very steep angle of attack. Instead, you swing the club back low and forward in a long sweeping arc. A pitching wedge on the other hand, because of its shorter shaft, is swung back more uprightly and through in a more descending blow.

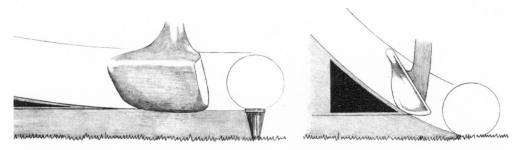

THE ANGLE OF ATTACK *for any golf shot relates directly to the length of the club being swung.*

Knowing what happens to make a ball go high or low helps you understand flight patterns. If we could see that ball being hit in a frame by frame photograph, we could understand why the ball goes higher with a wedge than a 3-iron. The additional loft of the wedge club allows the ball to slide or crawl up the face of the club higher and, therefore, leave

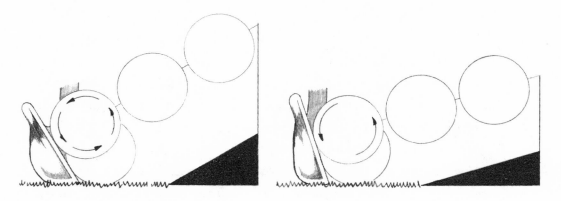

A LESS-LOFTED CLUB FACE *will produce a shot with a lower trajectory.*

the clubface on a steeper trajectory. All well struck shots, we have already said, hit the ball below its equator. A ball crawling up the face of a 3-iron does not leave the clubface at a very steep trajectory so the flight is less high.

For players who hit the ball high, such as Jack Nicklaus, their swing patterns incorporate an upright swing plane and a steeply descending downswing. A player whose tendencies are to hit the ball lower would use an angle of attack that was less steep.

CENTERNESS OF HIT

One final physical law that influences all three properties is centerness of hit. Physicists call it hitting the percussion point. Golfers call it hitting the sweet spot. The facts are that the closer you come to hitting the ball with the exact center of percussion, which by the way isn't the center of the clubface, the more ''pure'' your shot will be. The percussion, or sweet spot, on a golf club is slightly off center toward the shaft side of the club-face. Because the clubhead itself is so small and you are trying to create so much clubhead speed in the swing it is virtually impossible to control hitting the ball on the sweet spot.

THE ''SWEET SPOT'' *of a club face is that spot which, when the ball strikes it, produces the truest shot.*

But don't misunderstand me. I didn't say you couldn't learn to hit the ball on the sweet spot. I just said you couldn't make yourself do it every time! Good, sound set-up fundamentals and a repeating swing pattern will contribute to at least coming close to hitting the sweet spot with every shot. And hitting the ball on that spot not only insures getting maximum distance from the shot, it significantly increases your chances of hitting the ball straight and with true trajectory. And not only that . . . it just feels so good! The ball feels like a feather and it makes you wonder why you can't do it every time.

The fact of the matter is that you can't do it every time because you are a human being and not a machine. Only machines have mechanically pure and correct swings every time. But the more you work and learn and practice, the more lessons you take and coaching you get from a qualified golf professional, and the more you *want* to improve, the better you will get.

Understand these basic physical laws and how they influence what

EVEN THOUGH *there seems to be an endless number of things that can go wrong with a golf shot, in reality there are only nine directions the ball will go.*

happens when you hit a golf ball. Even though there seems to be endless combinations of things that can go wrong with your golf game there really are only a few possibilities for a golf ball's flight. It can go too short, too long, or just right! It can go too high, too low, or just right! And it can go in one of only nine directions as illustrated here. Luckily for us, because we are human beings and not machines, we don't always have to have *everything* perfect to hit a playable golf shot. As Mary Lou Crocker, an LPGA Tour veteran once said, ''The game is made up of misses. But it's better to miss it toward your target than to miss it not toward your target!''

Learning to accept those playable misses is another facet of using your head in golf that we will get to a little bit further on. Right now let's take your understanding of these physical laws and move forward with your physical learning of the necessary fundamentals to make them work.

CHAPTER THREE
Pre-Swing Fundamentals

When you start out to learn or improve your golf swing you must have a plan. Sports psychologist Dr. Linda Bunker puts it this way, "Failing to plan is planning to fail." Not only is this true in playing the game, it's also true in learning the swing. Most people approach a golf swing as though it's something to be completed in the shortest amount of time possible. The other extreme are the folks who seem to fall asleep over the ball. Maybe they may be praying the shot will work out for all I know.

But a good plan, I think, is to realize that there are two phases to hitting a ball. The first phase is your pre-swing phase. That is followed by the in-swing phase. Sometimes we are so busy trying to think of everything we're doing in the in-swing phase that we forget to plan well during the pre-swing part. That's a deadly error!

There are three very necessary fundamentals in the pre-swing phase: grip, aim and set-up. All of these things can be done before any action takes place. And all of them ultimately have a tremendous effect on the action that will take place. Let's examine each of them in detail so that you can improve your skill in these important areas.

GRIP

I feel strongly that the absolute first thing you have to master is a good grip on the golf club. Think of it! It is your only connection with that implement. Can you imagine a pianist trying to play a symphony without first learning the home positions for his hands on the piano? Hardly! But millions of golfers still try to play this game with what feels like a "natural" grip. I call it the "hamburger-ham sandwich grip!" Target side hand on the club in pretty good position but the rear hand, the right one for right-handers and left for left-handers, is usually way under the club shaft. Although that feels very comfortable at address, it is very inefficient — in fact, downright wrong, when the club in motion comes back to hit the ball.

With one hand facing north and the other facing west it is impossible for any golfer to make the two hands work as a single unit. They will, instead, work as opposing forces and the natural release that occurs in a good swing will be affected . . . not to mention the flight of the ball.

If you keep in mind that the only purpose of the grip is to hold on to the club in a way that allows the golf swing itself to bring the clubface through the ball in a square position, then you can understand the importance of positioning your hands in a way that is mechanically correct.

Keep it simple for yourself. But understand that simple doesn't necessarily mean it will be easy. If you have never used a correct grip, it will seem uncomfortable and totally wrong. You will feel like you can never hit a ball with your hands on the club in that position. But stop and ask yourself, do you see any modern day tour players using a poor grip? No, because they know the only way is the right way.

Sure, there have been players who had bad grips. Walter Hagen had an inefficient grip. And he paid for it by not being as consistent in his long game. Compared to some of the other players of the day he really sprayed the ball around. Miller Barber had a different grip for awhile, but then many things in Miller's game look different. The fact is that at impact everything works.

Making the two hands work as one unit means positioning them on the club so they are facing each other. Let your hands and arms hang loosely by your side. How do they hang in this natural position? They hang with the thumbs ever so slightly to the inside, toward your body. Nobody's arms hang with the palms facing out or up. To allow the arms and hands to work most efficient and most naturally throughout the swing pattern the hands should be placed on the golf club close to the way they hang. Palms facing. Thumbs ever so slightly inward. And to make them work as a unit they should be placed close together.

Check your fingernails. By that I mean that when you have a proper golf grip you should only see the thumbnail of your right hand. When you see a whole gang of nails on that right hand, you know you have the club down in the palm of the right hand instead of more into the fingers as it should be.

Check the V's formed between your forefingers and thumbs. It's an old checkpoint but it's still valid. If the V of the left hand is pointing off over the right shoulder and the V of the right hand is too, then you don't have a good grip. Both V's should be pointing to the center or left of your throat.

And don't have spaces where you can see the club grip between the two hands. How you choose to put them together so that they make a snug unit is a matter of personal preference. It's one of those things you will learn about yourself and your game during those five years I believe it takes to really learn how to play.

There are three accepted ways of combining the hands into a single unit: the ten-finger grip, the interlocking grip, and the relatively new overlapping grip. And the fact that successful players have used any one of the three lets you know that one is not necessarily better than the others. However, one may be better than the others FOR YOU.

The ten-finger grip, sometimes called the ''baseball grip,'' in which the two little fingers simply lie side by side on the club, is probably the least popular of the three. Part of the reason for that is that many people

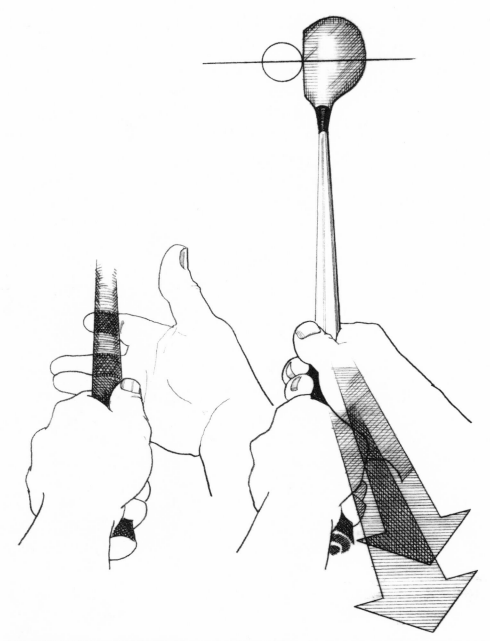

FOR THE HANDS TO WORK AS A UNIT *in golf the palms must face each other and the V's formed between the forefinger and thumb should point in the same direction.*

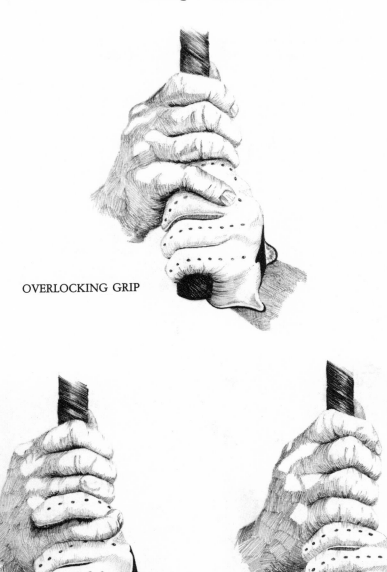

OVERLOCKING GRIP

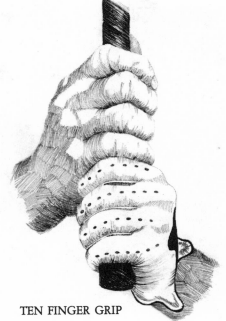

INTERLOCKING GRIP

TEN FINGER GRIP

CHICK EVANS *was a proponent of the ten finger grip.*

have trouble making the hands work together unless they are actually joined in some way. Chick Evans was the first American professional to play successfully with the ten-finger grip. More recently Bob Rosburg also used it.

While you may not choose the ten-finger grip as your playing grip it can sometimes be used in practice in a drill situation. By hitting a few balls with this grip you can sometimes begin to feel the clubhead a little better. You can feel the toe turning through the swing rather than holding on to the club so tightly that no release occurs.

The interlocking grip has been used for centuries as a tried and true method of joining the hands into a unit. I believe this grip has the tendency to keep your hands closer together with less slippage. Sometimes, if you find yourself getting blisters on the sides of your fingers, you know your grip has been slipping during the swing.

Jack Nicklaus started out with an interlocking grip, then experimented for a while with an overlapping grip. He came back to the interlocking grip because he said he felt his hands had a tendency to slip using the overlapping.

The classical interlocking grip, used with a lot of wristiness when hickory shafts were being swung, actually had the left thumb off the shaft sort of behind the right hand. Gene Sarazen was probably the last great player who used that full interlocking grip. The more modern interlocking grip of today has the left thumb on the shaft, under the right palm in a manner similar to the ten-finger and the overlapping grips.

The overlapping grip is the most modern of the three. It is generally thought to have originated with Harry Vardon and is sometimes called the Vardon grip. Like every other successful player of the early twentieth century, Vardon was primarily self-taught. He reported that he arrived at an overlapping grip after trying every other grip he had ever heard of. When he devised it, not only was the little finger of the right hand overlapped, or as he called it "riding" on the first finger of the left unique, but

IN HIS HEYDAY *Gene Sarazen played with the classical interlocking grip.*

it was also different to put the hands so snuggly together that the right hand totally covered the left thumb on the top of the grip.

What Vardon said about his "new" grip in 1905 might be said for any golfer still today: "The success of my grip cannot be guaranteed at the first trial. It needs some time to become thoroughly happy with it."[1]

One thing I *can* guarantee. If you will take the time to learn the correct position for your hands on the golf club, or if you will take the time to *re*-learn the correct position if you now have an incorrect one, you will be one step closer to having a repeatable golf swing. If you do not want to make this change or do not want to take the time to learn it correctly from the beginning, then you have little chance for consistency in golf.

If you do not have a lot of strength in your hands and arms, you may have to modify the position *slightly*. Many women, because the female body does not have as much upper body strength as the male's, may not have very strong hands and arms. Some senior citizens may have lost some grip strength. If this is the case you may have to shift your grip . . . that is BOTH hands . . . in a slightly clockwise direction. But a general rule of thumb is that when you look down at the grip you should never see more than three knuckles on the back of your left hand. And, of course, the right hand should still be facing the left, having also slightly shifted.

Another thing that you may not have given much thought to is the amount of pressure or tension in your grip. But that is every bit as important as the position or placement of the hands.

If you don't believe it just try this experiment. Hold a golf club very loosely in your grip. Have a friend hold the clubhead end of the club. Without telling you when he's going to do it, have your friend try to twist the club. You will see that the club turns in a grip that is too loose. Try the other extreme. Hold on as tightly as possible. This time your friend

---

[1]. Vardon, Harry. THE COMPLETE GOLFER, New York: McLure, Phillips, 1905.

will not even be able to turn the toe of the club over at all. That should be proof enough that a grip that is entirely too tight will severely hamper the proper ''release'' of the golf club during the swing.

What, then, is the correct pressure? I can't tell you. And neither can any other teacher of the game. Feel must be developed. But I can tell you this: I believe that a firm grip gives you more control of the club. You are the only person who can feel difference between firm and tight. Tight kills a swing, firm controls a swing.

Check yourself to see if you are getting ready to hit the ball with your shoulders all ''up tight'' and hunched up. If so, you can't help but be tight in your grip because it tranfers right down through the arms to the hands. Practice a few swings back and forth making sure that your shoulders are relaxed. Stretch your shoulders down from your ears. Let the arms swing and feel the grip relax to that firmness that allows you to hold onto the club without strangling it to death! Remember the force of the swing is going to make your grip tighten naturally. Don't start out so loose that it becomes a ''grab'' or so tight that it becomes so rigid the clubhead never releases.

Again we come right back to the need of every individual to spend some time learning not only the fundamentals of the game, but also learning about their own bodies and minds. You have to hit balls, have instruction and hit *more* balls to improve in golf. You have to learn how to position your hands on the club. And then, you have to stop and check that position every few shots to make sure you haven't lost it.

You have to stop and consciously feel how tightly you're hanging onto the golf club. If it's too tight, then you have to make yourself relax the muscles of the shoulders and arms before swinging again. If your grip is too tight in practice, you can imagine what it will be like during competition or when you have that long carry over a lake? Getting to recognize a certain feel in your grip . . . that takes time. But it is time well spent.

And, luckily for those of us who have busy schedules that do not permit practice at the golf course every day, we can practice assuming the correct grip sitting right at a desk or in the living room. And we can tune into the amount of pressure we are using to grip the club without having to hit a single ball.

AIM

The second pre-swing fundamental that you must master is better practiced at the driving range than in your living room. But I am constantly amazed at how many golfers, even experienced ones, seldom, if ever, practice aiming. They just hit the ball out there anywhere, sometimes making the worst swing errors to get it to go to where *they think* they're aiming!

You see professionals playing for a living taking considerable time in aiming every shot they hit. Sure your aim for a drive out into a wide-open fairway can be more general than the aim of a five-foot putt, but both shots had better be directed at *some* target.

If you accept the idea that golf is a target game, and it is, then you need to always work with a target in mind. Learning to be a marksman is not so much practice in the mechanical technique of squeezing a trigger as it is in aiming the rifle BEFORE squeezing the trigger. Golf is not so very different.

The fundamental of aim is really a two part idea. A lot of people confuse the two parts and that leads to some poor skills in this area. Aiming in golf is a combination of aiming the swing through the ball and aiming the body itself. And because it is difficult to have both the target side shoulder (the left for most people) plus the ball and clubface BOTH going toward the target, people get confused. Some people will try to aim their shoulder at the target. Others will try to aim the clubface at the target. What is right?

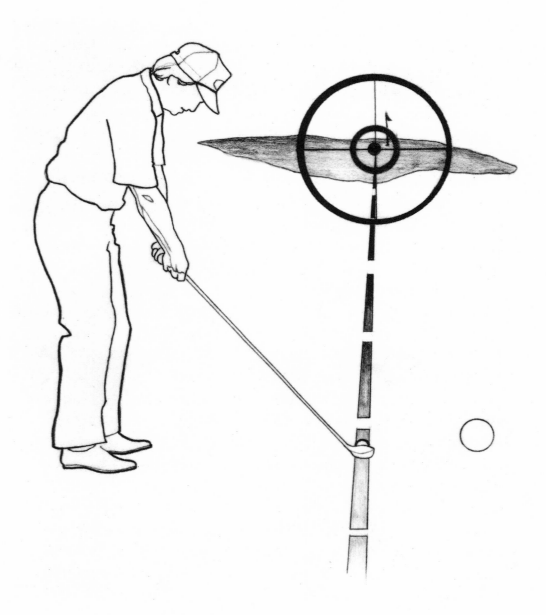

EVERY SHOT *in golf should be directed at some target.*

Because you expect to hit the ball to the target you should aim the clubhead to the target. It's that simple. Once the clubface is set up square to the target, that is with the bottom or sole edge of the clubhead at a right angle to the target line, the body can be aimed *along a parallel line* to the target line. If you are a right handed golfer, your body will be aimed parallel left of the target line; if you are left handed, you will be aimed parallel right of the target line.

Now that you know what to aim where, let's look at how you will go about it. If we could do a good job of aiming while standing in the address position, then you would see marksmen shooting, rifles held out beside them. Instead, marksmen put their eye behind the barrel and aim down the barrel. Golfers have got to do the same thing.

Even though you may have a pretty good idea of your target line from beside it, it is only when you stand behind the ball that you can see the total picture of aim. Chances are the first few times you try this technique of aiming you will feel like you are way off target when you look up after taking your address position. That goes right back to what we were just talking about. Your body *is* off the target line and your eyes are in your body, not on the ball or clubface.

If you watch today's good players, amateurs and PGA and LPGA tour stars, you will see they all have their own specific routine for standing behind the ball and aiming it. Many of them, Jack Nicklaus among them, often use an intermediate target to help them aim more consistently. I would suggest that you use one too, at least until you are absolutely secure in your aiming technique. And even then remember, aim and alignment are those fundamentals that most often seem to slip away without practice and periodic checking.

To use an intermediate target you simply need to learn to spot different colors in the grass or to locate a divot or some other recognizable ''spot'' close to the golf ball on the target line. Then, instead of having to work with the distant target you can work with soling your club so that it faces that spot, the intermediate target.

An additional advantage of using an intermediate target is that it allows you to better visualize your target line after the club is correctly soled. You can almost see a line between the spot and the ball itself. Then it's easy to line yourself up parallel to it.

Research available today shows us that lining up our bodies parallel and square to the target line is the most efficient way to play a shot we plan to go straight. But I've seen many great players use different kinds of body aim or alignment. Tommy Armour always set up with his body closed to the target line. By closed I mean that his left foot was brought up closer to the target line than the right foot. And Armour, like anyone else setting up with a closed alignment, hit the ball from right to left with a hooking flight to the ball.

Not many players today use that type of stance, but you do occasionally see someone like Lee Trevino who sets up with his body *seemingly* aimed well to the left or open to the target line. And, as is the case with most open body alignments, Lee hits a left to right ball. But we all know that Lee is a masterful artist of the game and even he probably doesn't know EXACTLY how he does what he does. As I've said before, some people just have a lot of talent and can use more variety in their technique. Most of us can't, particularly when there's not a lot of time for practice and play on a regular basis.

Aiming or aligning the body takes a little bit more attention than we are sometimes willing to give it. I've seen many golfers simply place their feet on a parallel line to the target line and fire away. Then they wonder why the shot didn't fly straight. The human body is not a rigid, single-piece unit so it's possible for different body parts to be aimed in all sorts of directions. The foot line is only one part to be aligned or aimed. You also have to keep the hips squarely facing the target line and you have to keep your shoulders facing the target line. Any one of those three being opened or closed can spell disaster for your swing. I remember seeing Jack Nicklaus practice at the 1974 U.S. Open at Winged Foot with his shoulders aligned extremely closed. They were on a line so far right of his target that it was virtually impossible for him to hit the shot anywhere near his intended target. Even though it's hard to make changes during a competition, I told Jack where his swing path (remember that is directly related to the shoulder position at impact) was "aimed" . . . due right! And while he didn't change it immediately, we did work on the position after that Open. An abrupt change in mid-tournament might have done more harm than good and, as it turned out, Jack went on to finish respectably in a 10th place tie in the tournament. (That brings up a point you might want to remember when you take your new game into competition. That will be neither the time nor place to tinker with your swing. It *must* be done before or after on the practice tee if you are going to enjoy consistency.)

If you think you're the only one to have ever felt awkward when you change something with your grip or aim or anything else in your game you'll be glad to know that Jack HATED the new position with his shoulders square or even a little open to his target line. He protested just like you do when asked to change. But the results, a more efficient swing with shots straight down the middle, convinced him that even though he *felt* like all he was going to do was hit it left, he was in the correct position to hit it straight down the middle.

Just one final thing about aiming: the "science" of aiming is done from behind the ball, lining it up to the target; the "art" of aiming is done when you take time for that look down the fairway or down the putting line to the target. After you get all the mechanics taken care of and the clubface/ball is aimed and the feet/hips/shoulders are all in line parallel, then you look up to see where you want to direct that free swing pattern you're about to make.

This is *not* the time to start fidgeting around and changing anything. I know it may not look "right." But you have already set up technically correct, so it *is* right. If you have doubts have a buddy stand behind you to check your aim. And when you practice, put a club down parallel to your target line so you can feel yourself squarely facing that club and you can direct your swing down a line parallel to it. Make yourself practice and practice until *you* believe that what you see when you look up at the address position is correct. You should feel like you have to sort of swing out toward that target.

But a word of caution here. If you are a golfer who has been aiming to the right for a long time you have probably been compensating by swinging from the outside to the inside to make the ball go to the left . . . thereby going toward your target. That's the old idea of putting together two wrongs to make a right.

Now when you correct your aiming problem you will get a mixed signal. When you look up from the address position at your target, it will seem like you are aiming well to the left of it, just like it seemed that way for Jack Nicklaus. If your swing pattern continues to be one of outside-to-inside, you can then REALLY convince yourself that you're aimed all wrong because the ball will go far left of your target. Here's where some good professional instruction can really help you. If that's not possible, then by all means use that club lying on the ground parallel to your target line for practice and MAKE yourself swing along that line. Try to hit the ball well right of your target. You'd be surprised how that may land your shot right on target.

So use the "art" of aiming, too. See where you want to direct your swing. Look at where you want the ball to go. Visualize the shot going out there perfectly. And then just let 'er go! But before you're ready to move on to the actual swing fundamentals, there is one more area of pre-swing fundamentals that you must master if you're to have the best chance of making a successful swing pattern.

SET-UP

The third fundamental of getting ready to swing is the way you position your body for the swing. That includes a number of different, but related, areas. And to be a good player you have to learn to mentally run through your list of set-up checkpoints. Set-up includes your total body position, what kind of stance you use, where you put your body weight, how you bend or don't bend your body. And it also includes how you relate to the golf ball, where it is in your stance and how far away from it you stand.

Without a good set-up your body will never be in a position to make a good efficient golf swing. Again, it's as simple as that! Having taken a fundamentally sound grip on the club and having gone through your aiming procedure, you're now ready to position the body. The question comes up, "Position the body WHERE . . . and HOW?" How can you tell if the body is in a position that is correct for your physique, your height and other physical characteristics?

Keep it simple. How would you stand if you were playing another sport that required you to move? How would you stand if I were to come up to you and push against your sternum or breast bone as if I wanted to push you over? You'd spread your feet far enough apart to keep your balance. For men that's about shoulder width, for women, who often have narrow shoulders but wider hips, about hip width. And you'd have to let your knees relax with your weight more or less on the balls of your feet to keep me from pushing you over. But watch out that you don't get too far up on the balls of the feet or you'll topple out over your target line in the swing. Instead keep your weight just into the instep side of the balls of your feet, letting a little of it be on the instep edge of the heels. Divide the weight about 50-50 between the left and right feet.

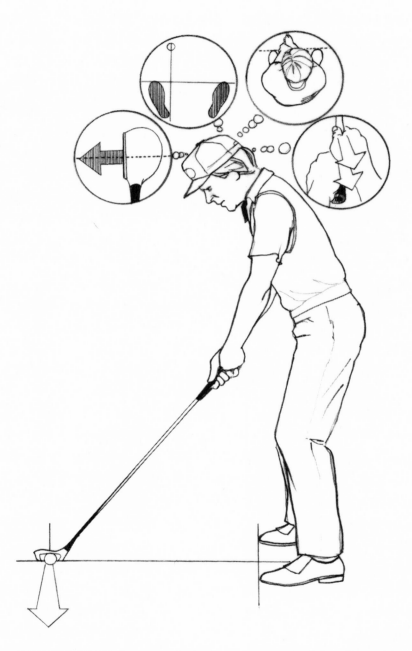

RUN THROUGH *the set-up checkpoints to ensure the right swing position.*

Since part of your objective in making your best golf swing is to create the biggest swing arc possible, you will want to make sure you don't bend over too much. On the other hand, standing too upright makes it impossible to create ANY kind of swing arc. Think about your bend as coming more at the hips than at the waist. If I came up poked you with a club on the top of the thigh right where your legs join your body that's where you should bend. And the bend will be just what would happen if I pushed you up and back with that club. The backside does not tuck in and under. If it does, you're going to be in the way of your own downswing. Instead the buttocks will simply be down and slightly out, allowing plenty of room for the hands and arms to swing freely through the thigh area. The back will stay straight but will be tilted because of the bend at the hips.

Without a lot of experience it may be hard for you to feel the set-up position. Working on it in front of a mirror will help you see correct positioning of the body parts.

Once you have a feeling for the correct position of the lower body, you will need to have a checklist for the upper body as well. When we talked about the grip, we mentioned the necessity of keeping unnecessary muscular tension out of the shoulders and arms. Therefore, the set-up position must be a relaxed one with the target side, or left arm, straight but not stiff. This concept of the straight left arm is a fairly new one in the game. Players well into the 20th century allowed their arms to bend severely during the backswing. Harry Vardon was particulary known for that arm position.

But modern research has shown that adding that bend at the elbow joint simply adds another variable for us to deal with. It's better not to have to deal with anything extra. But before you encase that left arm in plaster try this: Hold your left hand up by your left ear. Now swing your left arm across your body and out to your left side WITHOUT

CHAPTER THREE

STRAIGHTENING YOUR LEFT ARM! Pretty hard to do, isn't it? The force of a swinging motion makes the arm want to straighten. That's all well and good if you do make a good swinging motion with the golf club. But if you want to hit that ball with the right hand, then you can't count on the left arm straightening back out to a predictable and repeatable position. So it just makes more sense to keep it relaxed but straight in the set-up.

Another thing that makes more sense is to keep the right shoulder a little lower than the left at set-up. Becauses the right hand is lower on the golf club than the left this is a natural position. By keeping the shoulder lower but the weight divided evenly between the left and right you are in position that encourages a good takeaway. That's the whole idea of any set-up position . . . to make it easy to start the swing out correctly.

And with the right shoulder lower you will find it easy to have the head predominantly behind the ball. This head position is desirable because it's where you want to be at impact, not out in front of the ball with the body lunging toward the target. Set up there to make it easy to return there. It's all fundamental.

A quick word of caution here. In setting up with the right shoulder slightly lower and the head behind the ball it could be easy to allow the hand position to lag behind the ball as well. This is *not* what you want to do. We know some of the great classical players dragged the hands back with the clubhead following. Even Bobby Jones did that most of his career. But we come right back to today's more modern and more mechanically efficient golf swing. The set-up for this swing keeps the hand position more in line with that straight left arm. This means the hands will be slightly ahead of the clubhead at address. *Slightly* ahead, now, not way ahead with half the loft of your clubface removed because it has been placed in a hooded position. Any positioning of the hands must make you aware of simply placing the clubhead fully on its sole and square to the target line. Too much pushing the hands ahead can lend to opening the clubface, too.

Having now carefully considered both the positioning of your body and the posture of your body, let's review the placement of the ball. Those three ''P's'' are all part of the set-up. The placement of the ball must be considered both in terms of how far away from your body it's placed and where, within the stance, it is placed.

How far away from your body is largely determined by the club you have selected. But I've seen many a person on my lesson tee with the ball so close to themselves they can't swing or so far away they have to reach for it. My feeling is simply this: If you have good body posture it's hard to get too far away or too close! It's all related to how you ''hang'' your shoulders out toward the ball and how you bend your hips. And, vice versa, they are both related to how far away from the ball you stand. It's a little bit of that chicken and egg theory.

The simplest way I can tell you to find out how far away from the ball you should stand with any club is to stand upright holding the club out in front of you, horizontally. Keep both arms extended. Then tilt or bend at the hips allowing the backside to stay more out than tucked in. While you're doing this keep the upper arms close to the chest. Don't keep them scrunched in so tightly that you produce muscular tension, but keep them in slight contact with the sides of the chest. As you allow yourself to settle into your set-up position with the knees flexed, bring the clubhead down to where it is properly soled on the ground. That basically is where the ball should be played by you, with that club.

We go back to ''feeling'' so many times in this game. The feeling of this set-up is that the arms are lightly hanging off the shoulders. In fact a good checkpoint to see if your shoulders are out and away from your hips far enough to swing is to simply drop the club from your hands when you are in your set-up position. Allow the arms to hang freely. They should not touch your thighs.

Even though you may be comfortable and correct with the distance you stand from the ball, you still must pay close attention to where the ball is in the stance. That can really play havoc with the golf swing! You can get into trouble in either direction with this one. To my way of thinking, you can get into more trouble with the ball too far back in your stance than you can with the ball too far forward.

Where YOU play the ball is primarily related to how lively your golf swing and your footwork are. Think of it this way: The fellows and ladies who once played with whippy hickory shafts had to rely on a lot of hand action to slap that club through. So they had to move the ball around in the stance so it would be in a position to be struck before the turf with whatever length club they were using. A longer club called for a forward ball placement; a short club meant you had to move it back somewhat.

But we've moved to more modern shafts and found out that these swing mechanics you're learning right now contribute to a driving, swinging motion, so we have established a more consistent pattern of ball placement; driver off inside of left heel so that it can be hit a slightly ascending blow; fairway woods, inside of left foot; irons, slightly ahead of center.

I said earlier I think you can get into more trouble keeping the ball too far back. But sometimes, particularly if you're not using much leg drive in your swing because of some limitation, or if you just swing in a more classical, "armsy" manner, you will have better results with your shortest irons, nine and the wedges, by playing them just to the center or behind the center of your stance. The bottom line for your ball position is to put it in a position where you will hit the ball before the turf WHILE MAKING A GOOD SWINGING MOTION. The last part is important because you don't want to get into the habit of just moving the ball around to make up for a poor swing pattern.

In fact, having that ball too far back can add to your tendencies to slap at the ball from a flat-footed position. It can keep you from hitting the ball straight, adding to your tendencies to hit it out to the right. And, of course, it will contribute to your hitting the ball lower than your normal trajectory.

Probably the greatest player who placed the ball back in his stance for all shots was Tommy Armour. But there was a reason. Tommy had lost an eye during World War I so he needed the ball back there for perception. But even the great timing and terrific hands of Tommy Armour did not modify the physical laws . . . he hit the ball very low! His tremendous coordination made it possible for him to close his stance, use his hands, and play the ball in a right to left flight pattern.

On the other hand, if you have the ball too far forward in the stance you can also develop some swing problems. The good thing about keeping that ball up front in a good position like all of the modern professionals do is that it makes it easy to get the ball in the air. But getting it too far up can make you lose distance because it goes too high.

A second problem with having it too far forward is that you may change your body position to facilitate playing the ball. To get the club on the ball you will open your upper body to the target line. The left shoulder can be pulled back away from the target line and that can make you either pull the shot left or, more likely, hit a glancing blow that produces a slice.

Starting your set-up by putting both feet together with the ball placed between them is the surest cure for having the ball either too far back or forward. From that position simply step toward the target a few inches with the left foot and then step away from the target as many inches as necessary with the right foot. For a driver you would step further back with the right than you would for an eight-iron. Using this technique can be helpful when you suspect that the ball position is playing havoc with your play during a round, too.

As you step into your set-up position there is one more little thing to be aware of. I like to see a player set up with the left toe turned out a little bit. It will simply make it easier to transfer and balance the weight on that side at the end of the swing. It makes it easier to turn the hips back to that side. So why not do it?

There was one great player who defied even that position. An English professional by the name of Henry Cotton, who won three British Opens, played absolutely pigeon-toed! Both feet turned inward. But he was the only one I ever knew who did that. Even today you'll see people playing with both toes turned out at the set-up. I still prefer to keep the right foot pretty much at right angles to the target line and the left toe a little out.

SUMMARY

We have spent more than a little time on these fundamentals of "getting ready." They are not too exciting, I'll admit. Most people want to just stand up there and rip at the ball. That's more exciting. The only problem is that they have to "rip at it" so many times before their round is over! And nobody ever "tore up a golf course," in the parlance of the players, with too many rips.

Taking the time to master a good grip, a correct aiming technique, and a sound set-up routine is something that any golfer can do. You do not have to be inordinately skilled. You don't have to have fine-tuned coordination. You do not have to be exceptionally strong . . . or flexible . . . or tall . . . or short . . . or ANYTHING EXCEPT PATIENT.

Learning the feel of the most efficient grip for you takes time. Learning to trust that feel takes even more time. Not going back to old habits under pressure takes still more time and concentration. But there is no one who has improved his or her golf game significantly without finally getting to a good contact point with the golf club.

Developing an aiming procedure that you repeat with every shot takes perserverance. Allowing the eyes to guide you in planning the swing takes practice. Believing it will work takes guts! But a smooth, confident swing can be made only when you are convinced that you're truly going to your target. An efficient swing can be made only when you are.

Creating an awareness of body position AND body posture AND ball placement takes meticulous planning. But all three are necessary in building a repeatable set-up from which a free-flowing swinging motion can be made. There are enough obstacles on the golf course. Why make your own body an additional one? Commit yourself to learning the facts AND feel of a good set-up position.

Once those three fundamental areas have become as important to you as learning to hook the ball or put action on a pitch shot, you will have come to grips with this game. No house stands that is not built on a strong foundation. Your pre-swing fundamentals are the foundation for your golf swing, and thereby your golf game. Spend enough time on your foundation so that your game will stand the ravages of courses, conditions, and competitions!

CHAPTER FOUR
Fundamentals of the Swing Itself

Now that the foundation has been properly laid for your swing it is time to examine those other fundamentals that make it work. They are simple to understand, but they take time to learn. They take practice to perfect. And they take professional evaluation and coaching to improve.

A golf swing is simply that . . . a SWING! It is not a hit, although the ball does get hit. And it is not a lunge, although the body weight does transfer from side to side. Instead, it is quite simply a swinging motion of the arms, assisted by other body parts, toward a target. As human beings, we persist in wanting to make it complex, but it isn't.

So let's move on to these fundamentals that will not only allow you to keep it simple, but will also allow you to make it repeatable. I think it should make perfectly good sense to you that if we can keep the concept of this swinging motion simple, then it will be much easier to make a repeatable, consistent swing. There are no gimmicks nor short cuts. There is only basic learning and then lots of practice and refinement.

I stressed in Chapter 2 how Jack Nicklaus uses his brain and good sense in this game. One of the ways he uses them is that he never stops learning and refining these fundamentals. You will do that same thing. And you will see continued growth in your skills from that learning, provided you make time to practice.

But what are you going to practice? One of the things you need to practice, or at least to be aware of, has more to do with getting ready to move than with actually moving. I'm talking about what you do to initiate your golf swing. It's hard enough to start a swing from a static set-up position as it is. Golfers I see who are too tense or thinking so hard about the mechanics of the swing that they can't start it smoothly have a difficult time creating a good move.

Any really skilled player you see, professional or amateur will always use something to get going. It becomes part of the pre-shot routine that we'll touch on more later in these lessons. What it is doesn't matter as much as what it DOES. And, that it is the SAME thing every time.

Many fine golfers use a waggling motion of the club with their hands and arms immediately before starting the backswing. I think this is fine,

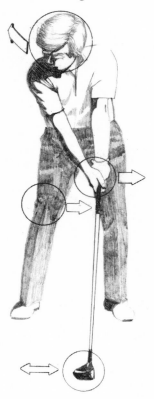

THE WAGGLE MOTION *acts as a rehearsal for the swing.*

but I don't like to see a golfer flopping the club back and forth, all wristy. Make that waggle, if you do waggle, away from the golf ball with the arms and wrists moving in a similar manner to your backswing move. After all, one of the reasons for using the waggle is as a muscular rehearsal.

Other golfers, like Gary Player, for example, sort of kick in the right knee toward the target. Again, it's a personal preference. This type of movement allows the backswing to sort of rebound from the knee kick and it also helps you to stabilize the weight on the inside of the right leg during the backswing.

Still others like to press the hands and club slightly forward as the swing trigger. This ''forward press'' is among the most popular moves you see tour players make. It's the theory of start slightly forward to then move back. And, executed properly without so much ''press'' that it changes the clubface position, it can serve to help insure the hands staying ahead of the clubhead.

Jack Nicklaus and Sam Snead both use yet another technique for starting the swing. Immediately before taking the club back, they will turn their heads slightly to the right. Jack says he ''swivels his chin.'' This move not only starts the action, it also allows a complete shoulder turn and helps to keep the head behind the ball at impact. Done properly, this movement is on the shoulder line. That is why it is more of a swivel than a turn.

Whatever movement or movements you choose, they should serve to ready the body and to relax muscles *without* undoing anything you have already done in your set-up. Also they should provide a smooth transition from the static position at set-up to the dynamic movement of the swing.

While the entire swing usually takes less than two seconds to execute, we need to take considerably more time to examine the basic fundamentals necessary to make it work. Let's look at the important ones right now.

CHAPTER FOUR

FULL AND COMPLETE EXTENSION

If you accept the basic fact that the golf swing is a swing, then it should be obvious that a swing extends. Think about a youngster on a playground swing. How does he or she get the biggest swing? They try to go higher and higher, don't they? But, the swing goes not only up, but OUT also. If it didn't, the child would be dumped out pretty early on the back part of the swing.

That's exactly what will happen to you if you don't fully extend the backswing of your golf swing; your power will be dumped out early in it! There are a number of things that contribute to extending the swing out and back, but the two basic ones are the relatively straight left arm and the full shoulder and hip turn.

We said back when we were learning and reviewing the set-up that the left arm should be more or less straight at address. From that position it is easy to swing it back still in a straight or extended position. But where I see a lot of golfers get into trouble is right there. Their first move is not a swing at all! It is a lift. If you lift up, you're likely to hit down. That is effective only if you're trying to hit to China . . . straight down!

Think about it for a minute. If your first move is not a swing, you're immediately in jail because this whole swing action lasts only two seconds. There is no way you can change to a swinging action at the top of your backswing to come through the ball in a correct manner unless you take it away from the ball in a correct swinging manner.

So, you think about not only having the left arm straight at the set-up, but also think about doing something active with it during the backswing. It doesn't just tense up and stay straight out in space. Instead, on the backswing the left arm actually EXTENDS and swings back pushing the club away from your head and neck. This will make the arc of the swing as wide as possible. But this can be done only from a correct set-up position in which the left arm is straight but not tense. If the arm is rigid

56

and tense, it will be extremely difficult to make it active.

This wide arc of the swing is precisely what you're trying to create. When the clubhead is traveling through a big wide arc, it gathers a great deal of clubhead speed and velocity. That equals distance!

I said that you definitely did not want to lift up the club with the right hand and arm. But what do we want that right side to do during the backswing? Again, it is simple. We want the right arm to move into a position to swing forward. To do that, all you have to do is to ALLOW it to bend. If you're lifting and pulling with that right arm, it won't bend correctly. but, if your primary force is one of swinging back with the left, then you can let the right elbow bend, always pointing back and down, not out horizontally. Notice I did not say anything about keeping it close to your body. That's a matter of your own personal preference.

If you are young and flexible and swing on an upright plane, then your right elbow will move well away from the body during the backswing. Although he is swinging on a slightly flatter plane now, Nicklaus has always had that position with the elbow well away from his side. The checkpoint for him as well as for you is that the elbow points mostly down and somewhat behind you. Incidentally, one of the most vivid examples of keeping the elbow tucked close to the body, which forces the left arm and shoulder around in a flatter plane, is the swing of Ben Hogan. Obviously, from Jack's and Ben's records, both positions work. You will need to determine which one is best for you.

But there is more to extension than just swinging the arms back, up, and around. That arm swing is a trigger for starting the shoulders and hips turning. And when they turn, you get even more power to create clubhead speed.

Just like the old song says, "The arm bone's connected to the shoulder bone. . ." So, if that is true, it would seem that it would be natural for you to go ahead and turn the shoulders around as you swing the arms.

Well, it is, but golfers sometimes won't allow it to happen.

There are lots of reasons why this action is prevented but none are more obvious than poor posture at set-up. We keep going right back to the foundation. If it isn't laid properly, then you will find the entire swing is affected.

The second most common reason golfers can't (or don't) make a good shoulder turn is that they are in such a hurry to "hit" the ball that they do not give themselves enough time to complete the turn. Shoulder and hip muscles are big muscles, much bigger than those in the hands and arms. They take more time to move and to stretch. A backswing that is so quick that you don't have time to complete your full extension is the backswing of a BAD swing.

Sometimes I see golfers who come to the lesson tee without a lot of flexibility. Adult men, as a group, are less flexible than either women or juniors. This can make it difficult to turn far enough, but with practice, flexibility can be increased. Often, it is not the flexibility that prevents a good move as much as it is poor techniques.

How much turn is enough? Well, the experts say the best golfers turn their hips about 45-50 degrees and their shoulders 90-110 degrees on a full swing. That's a lot of turn. However, most golfers don't have instruments to measure degrees of turn. Use a buddy or a mirror to help you evaluate your turn. Someone watching you is better, for you will usually have to move your head to see yourself in a mirror and that can change your position. Have a friend stand behind you to your right side, on your target line. Make your backswing. Your friend should be able to see any logo on your golf shirt, or where a logo would be. Now remember, if you have a good upright swing, the left arm may be covering the logo, but you get the idea.

Another checkpoint is to have your friend stand facing you, parallel to the target line. At the top of your backswing your friend should see the inside edge of your right shoulder blade. Yes, I said *right*!

For your own checkpoint you should try to bring the left shoulder under the chin to a position *behind* the golf ball. Unless you can get behind the ball with both the mass of the club and the mass of your body, you will have a hard time moving that mass through the ball toward the target.

We've pretty well dissected the shoulder turn during extension, but what happens to the hips during this? If you are not careful, the hips will create their own set of problems. A simple movement pattern will keep that from happening.

I said before that poor technique keeps many people from making a good shoulder turn. Incorrect hip movements can prevent a good shoulder turn. Correct hip movement is simply this: turn them as far away from the target as you can without letting the right knee straighten and lock or without letting the weight go to the outside of the right foot. Peggy Kirk Bell calls this turning action the "cutting away" of the hips because the right hip moves back away from the target line. It is not a lateral movement, it's a turn. And it all comes down to the basic fact that the more turn you get, the more extension and power you have. But like all good things, there can be too much of it. Another fundamental of the swing helps keep the turning action controlled.

STEADY HEAD

More golfers have lost power and created poor technique by trying to keep their head still than by almost anything else. But there are equal numbers of golfers who are inconsistent because they don't keep their head steady. Sound confusing? It isn't.

All athletes need some type of centering. Gymnasts would topple off balance beams without it. Tennis players would lose power on ground strokes without it. Golfers misshit shots without it.

The violent force of a golf swing has to swing around something. Trying to make a repeatable move in which the clubhead is traveling upwards of 100 mph without keeping *something* relatively centered and steady is ridiculous.

The head has long been the most obvious center for golfers. Even though we know the actual center of the swing is really somewhere in the chest area it is easier to think about the head as it relates to the body turn, weight shift, and swing.

Computer analyses show that even touring professionals' heads move — on the backswing. Allowing a *slight* movement (pros move about two inches) facilitates that good full turn we were talking about. But the problem I see in amateurs is that they want to move the head *forward* too. That won't work.

Here is the simplest way of looking at what the head CAN do and what it CANNOT do in an efficient golf swing.

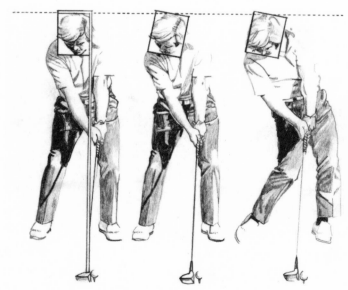

1. The head at set-up must be slightly behind the ball.

2. During the backswing motion the head must stay within the stance, that is, move no farther back than the **inside** *of the right foot.*

3. During the forward swing, the head must remain behind the ball position until after impact. It should then move forward and up to a relaxed finish of the swing.

So, as you see, it is not still, but it does stay pretty steady.

Probably the best player I ever knew who violated this fundamental was Walter Hagen. His head moved a great deal and he also had what I would call a bad grip. One or both of these dramatically affected his accuracy, particularly with long clubs. But once again his God-given talent more than made up for it. He could put that ball right at the pin from 100 yards in and hole putts from everywhere!

Another successful player who in his prime could sink putts from everywhere is Arnold Palmer. Noted for his exceptionally strong, active golf swing, Palmer has always had one of the absolutely steadiest heads in the game. That is one of the things which has allowed him to swing so hard.

Once you understand the necessity for having a steady head, you should practice maintaining it. Just like every other fundamental, it has to be practiced to be perfected.

One of the ways I help students learn what "steady" means is to place my hand or a club shaft near the right side of the head so they may feel when they move too far back. You can check yourself by swinging while looking at your shadow. Line up the shadow of your head with an object on the ground. Make your swing, keeping your head's shadow on or very near that object until after the bottom of your downswing.

This kind of drill can teach you the difference between keeping the head so still that you stifle your good turn and swing and simply keeping it steady enough to make a good swing.

But there's another steadying influence in the backswing, too. That's provided by the right leg. Proper weight shift and footwork make it easier to keep the weight balanced throughout the swing, never letting it slide to the outside of the right leg and foot.

CHAPTER FOUR

WEIGHT TRANSFER AND FOOTWORK

Although transfer of body weight to the right side and back to the left during the swing is related to both the swing of the arms and the turn of shoulders and hips, it is also very much related to the footwork within the swing. If you're like the majority of players I see at the lesson tee you probably haven't ever given much thought to what your feet do in this game.

Well, from over 50 years of experience I can tell you that they do a lot if you're a good golfer! And, if you're not so good yet, they probably aren't doing much of anything.

The set-up position from which the swing starts is one in which your body weight is pretty evenly distributed between left and right. And you're in a steady position on your feet. As you start your backswing, it becomes impossible to separate the extension of the arms, the turn of the shoulders and hips, and the shift of weight back to the right side into neat little specific movements.

You may be one of the golfers who has always heard that it's a three-part backswing with the hands moving, followed by the shoulders turning, followed by the hips and knees turning to transfer the weight. It's not nearly so segmented as that, nor should it be.

Let me give you an example of what I mean. If you hold a golf club in your left hand with the grip end pointing to the right and then transfer that club to your right hand, what part of the club moved first? Did the grip move before the shaft or before the clubhead? No, of course not. If it had, then the club would have had to stretch in length. But, in fact, the grip did LEAD the movement of the club to the right side. In the same way the hands pushing the club back LEADS the motion of the golf swing but all of the movements, the turning and tilting of the hips and the transfer of weight to the right side flow in a sequential continuing pattern of movement.

And, in the same way you would see the clubhead LEAD the movement if you were to pass the golf club back to your left hand, the movements of your downswing are started by moving the weight back to the left with the legs and hips moving back to target, a reversal of the order of the backswing. Again, it is a flowing, continuing movement pattern.

But let's get back to the fundamental weight shift that takes place during the backswing. The latest in computer analyses of the backswing show us that, in good golf swings, nearly 80% of the body weight has shifted to the right side by the time the golfer's hands have swung back to waist height. [1]Most of this happens because the hips and shoulders have started to turn. And as that happens the feet begin to play an active part.

The correct movement of the feet during the backswing, and forward swing, too, for that matter is one of rolling the ankles. The absolutely best in the world at doing this is Jack Nicklaus. If his mind is his best attribute in golf, his best physical skill is his footwork.

I first became aware of the importance of footwork in the golf swing in the 1930's. At the time I had gone to Hershey, Pa., to work for Henry Picard and to take lessons from him. Picard himself was also taking lessons, from an old fellow by the name of Alex Morrison, a really great teacher of the game. Morrison's "thing" was footwork and he himself was terrific at it. But Jack's better than Alex ever was; he's better than Jones, Hagen, Nelson, Hogan, or anyone else.

Because it is a simple fundamental, you too can become excellent at it by practice. A simple drill where you roll your left ankle inward while holding with the inside of your right ankle will help you learn the feeling. Then push of the right foot by rolling the right ankle to the left, shifting all the weight onto the left foot and raising the right foot up onto its toe.

[1] "The Bionic Swing," GOLF MAGAZINE. New York: Vol. 27, No. 6, June, 1985.

Be sure you are not simply lifting the left foot and lifting the right foot. Your left heel will come off the ground but it is *because of* the rolling of the ankle and it occurs in order to allow the hip to fully turn away to the right on the backswing. Some very flexible golfers can complete the weight shift and hip turn without allowing the left heel to lift but very few people can.

Notice how much pressure and actual muscular work occurs when you hold your weight on the inside of the right foot and leg. Many golfers do not ''work'' hard enough at stablizing and balancing the swing with this correct footwork. Remember that it will be impossible for you to keep the weight on the inside of the right foot if your shoulder turn or hip turn has moved outside your base of support, that is, moved outside the right leg. Keeping the head steady, the knees flexed and the ankles rolling all contribute to being able to make the fullest shoulder and hip turn without moving ''off the ball'' (outside your right leg).

To help yourself achieve the full turn while staying over your base of support you may want to practice making your turn with the proper roll of the left ankle toward the right side but without allowing the left heel to come off the ground. And remember that these footwork drills in which you practice a full rhythmic weight shift and turn can be done anywhere, without a golf club. In front of your mirror is a perfect place to practice and see what you are doing. Try with your eyes closed to get more of a kinesthetic feel for it. Feel how much time it takes you to roll the ankles and fully transfer the weight and complete your turn.

Tom Watson says that unless you can count to two you can't play golf. The full backswing doesn't happen in a half or quarter count; it takes the full ''1'' and the downswing takes the full ''2.'' Sam Snead always says the backswing should feel like you're swinging in maple syrup, unhurried and unrushed. Rolling your ankles and allowing the proper footwork to complement the hip and shoulder turn weight shift and arm swing is one way to insure good rhythm and balance within the backswing motion.

If footwork is important in the backswing portion of the golf swing, it is absolutely vital in the forward swing. Just as the shifting of a majority of the body weight to the right side occurred very early in the backswing phase, the shift back to the left side ocurs very early in the forward swing. That weight shift, and in fact the entire downswing, is started by the rolling and pushing of the right foot. The golf swing works from the ground up! It is not the knees turning, or the hips sliding or the arms swinging, it is the rolling and pushing of the right foot that starts the whole thing back toward the target.

That roll and push from the right to the left is what causes the knees and hips and shoulders to go toward the target in a lateral direction at first. This is what makes you feel a little like you're moving out toward right field in the downswing. But almost immediately the hips and shoulders start to unwind and turn, finishing with the body facing the target and the weight totally over on the left side.

If you do not interfere with the natural turning of the hips and shoulders, or try to force them to turn, you will feel them simply uncoil from the backswing position. As you can see, we just can't get away from that word ''feel.'' And that's what is so hard to develop.

Arnold Palmer has a greater turning on the backswing, so it looks like he spins his hips around more than some of the other players. Part of the reason goes right back to the individual talent that Palmer has and the tremendous strength he has in his upper body. He has great upper body action, while we see great leg action in Jack Nicklaus's swing, for example.

And although you can learn from watching them, you must get yourself up and practice and play and take your own lessons to develop the feel of the correct moves to make. Keeping in mind that footwork is the bottom line, no pun intended, will help you build the proper movement patterns for success.

CHAPTER FOUR

Remember all the while you're moving and turning back toward the target, the head stays slightly behind the ball until after impact. Speaking of impact, we've had you working and thinking so much about what the body is doing during this golf swing that we have sort of ignored the arms, hands and club. The last thing I had said about the swinging of the arms was that to make a full extension on the backswing you must feel like you are pushing the club back around and up, away from the neck. Let's go back and pick up the action and movements of the arms from that point in the backswing where you're trying to get good, full extension.

ARMS AND HANDS

As important as footwork, weight and shift and turn are to the swing, nothing is more important than the actions of the arms and hands. After all, nothing else has any contact with the golf club.

When we were discussing the grip I said that the hands are important for holding onto the golf club. Gripping the club is their greatest responsibility. They are not active "hitters" in the golf swing. Instead they are reactors to the swinging of the arms.

On the backswing the hands do not manipulate the club or forcibly cock the wrists. Instead the wrists cock quite naturally in reaction to the hinging or folding of the right elbow during the backswing. Most good golfers start the club swinging back along the same line they want to swing forward on. As the body coils and the shoulders turn, the right elbow will bend. This bending causes the wrists to cock. In fact it is almost impossible to bend this elbow and continue the shoulder turn without the wrists cocking.

If the elbow moves away from the body and into a high position the right wrist will automatically assume a good position in which the clubface remains square. On the other hand, if you keep the elbow close to the body and low, then the clubface can be open while going back and you will possibly lay the club off the line. Notice I didn't say you would do that consciously, just that it can be easy for it to happen. If it does, it will be necessary for you to add another move to close the clubface during the downswing. And then it is no longer the simplest move you can make.

Another factor that will help determine the position of the club and your wrists at the top of the backswing is your initial grip position on the club. Holding the club too much in the palm of the left hand will result in a left wrist position that is bowed at the top. Many golfers with weak hands seem to get into this position at the top, but it will also turn up in good players who may use it successfully. Lee Trevino is a good example. But it is an awfully complex position from which to swing the hands and should be avoided if possible.

Holding the club with the left hand on top of the grip, showing three or more knuckles at address, will result in a wrist position that is cupped at the top of the backswing. This, too, is not the most efficient position. If the hands are not manipulated back into a correct position before impact, a slicing swing is likely.

The desired position for the left wrist at the top is flat, or in line with the left forearm, neither cupped or bowed. This is the most efficient. It will very likely result if you swing your arms back and up into a position where the right elbow hinges and moves to a high position. Most modern tour players consider this ideal.

High speed cinematography shows that good players allow the total cock of the wrists to happen as the right elbow bends. They do not set their wrists early, which is a pretty unnatural move, nor do they cock them at the top of the backswing. It is true, though, that the weight of the clubhead at the top works to complete the wrist cock.

But waiting to set the hands at that late time during the swing is likely to result in either dropping the club below parallel by relaxing the grip or in ''casting'' or throwing the club forward in the early stages of the downswing. That means something has to be done actively to set the wrists. Allowing the bending of the right elbow to cock the wrists is much more natural and conducive to an uncomplicated swing.

And if the hands are ''quiet'' and nonactive in the backswing, it will be easier for them to remain that way in the forward or down swing. If they are not quiet and simply reactive at that time, you cannot possibly swing in the correct sequence of movement.

The early stages of the forward swing do not have the arms or hands doing anything but being pulled along by the body as it shifts the weight back to the target side and as the hips and upper body uncoil. By holding onto the club without excessive tension and by allowing the arms to swing freely forward in response to the body movements, you can keep the club in a vertical position during these early stages of the forward swing.

Many golfers use the hands throughout the swing but they should be using the arms and letting the hands react. Nowhere will this happen more than at the start of the forward swing.

Because the musculature of the hands is smaller, and thereby quicker moving, and because you sometimes are anxious to hit the ball, it is easy to start the hands forward first. No successful player has ever done that.

The great classical swings of the 20s and 30s didn't do that, even though they did use more arms and hands overall in the swing. Even if you can't use your legs and body as strongly as a young tour star, you still must keep the hands quiet and merely responsive at this stage of the swing.

It's fundamental and it's simple, but it takes practice to feel yourself doing it. Using half or short swings as a drill can help you feel how the hands are still as the swing starts down.

Going back to the mirror and watching your swing, trying to keep the hands and club in the same relative position to the forearms through the first stage of downswing as they were at the top of the swing can help you better visualize it in actual ball hitting practice. Jack Nicklaus had to practice this one fundamental for literally years before he learned to avoid this hitting tendency. You may have to work that long, too.

Just remember to work on good strong footwork and proper shifting of weight back to the left to initiate the downswing. If you consciously work to have certain body parts, in this case the rolling of the right ankle, do the correct move, then you'll have fewer problems keeping the wrong parts from trying to do it.

Some golfers concentrate on pulling the club down with their left arm. While it may help keep you from throwing the clubhead out with the hands, it won't necessarily help you make the correct move with your feet and body. A practice drill in which you start your backswing from an unnaturally narrow stance and then step toward the target with your left foot, rolling the right ankle as the first move of your downswing, also helps you feel the strong shift of body weight that must occur at that point in the swing.

Because you do hold onto the club with the hands, it is natural to want to hurry that club back to the ball WITH the hands. But not only do I see golfers who are prone to do that with the hands, some also want to rush the shoulders and arms forward too soon in the downswing. I think I've seen more weak slicing ball flights caused by overly quick shoulders, arms and hands than I've ever seen caused by spinning hips and legs.

Don't get me wrong. We all know that the more clubhead speed you generate, the further you'll hit the ball. But clubhead speed has never been or ever will be maximized by lunging through the impact area with the upper body. Instead, it is a matter of allowing centrifugal force to build up and unleash the clubhead through.

While that sounds really technical, it's really pretty simple. Think about ice skating. A line of skaters playing ''crack the whip'' has one skater at one end barely turning his body while the line circles. However, the skater out on the end, particularly if it's a fairly long line, is going like sixty! He's barely able to hang on, just flat flying around that circle. That's how your clubhead should be moving. And when you allow the weight shift and uncoiling of the hip and shoulder turn to swing the arms through the ball freely, it will be doing just that! But you notice the word there is "allow" not "make."

Swing a few times feeling the good footwork and weight shift on the forward swing. Notice that, when the body causes the arms to move rather than the arms causing the body to move your right elbow stays behind the right hip until very near impact. If your arms and shoulders are moving ahead of the feet and hips in the forward swing, the right elbow will move in front of the hip and the club then can no longer be moving down your target line. Instead, the club will be moving across the target line from outside of that line toward the inside of that line. And that will produce an undesirable ball flight, maybe a pull left or a slice right, depending on clubface position. It's hard even for professionals to plan to play a shot that might go either left or right!

IMPACT AND FINISH

No matter how different the swings of Bobby Jones, Miller Barber, Lee Trevino, Mickey Wright, Jack Nicklaus or any other successful player look from each other, they all look like peas in a pod at the time the club hits the ball. What I mean is that this is the moment of truth, for you as well as for them. Any variations and individual differences among fine players occur someplace either before or after impact. They all do pretty much the same thing at that moment. By practicing your fundamentals and knowing what it is you're trying to achieve, you, too can be consistent at impact. And because impact occurs during the swing, not at the end of it, you can go ahead and finish looking good enough to be on the cover of your favorite golf magazine.

"Hitting" the golf ball comes as yet another reaction to good techniques falling in line. We've just said how impossible it is to make your hands actively hit in a repeating manner. But what does happen at that all-important time?

Mechanically, what actually happens and what you will *feel* like happens may be two different things. Your feeling will be as if you're trying to swing the club as far as possible down the fairway. Sort of like you're trying to throw a frisbee with the left hand. In other words, you'll feel like you're really stretching out toward that target, swinging the club well past your left toe on the target line, or even feeling a little right of the target line. And while you're doing this, you'll have to feel your head staying behind the ball even though the weight has already shifted well to the left side. A young, supple person can do and feel this pretty easily. Most of the rest of us are going to have to attempt to do it the best way we can without giving up too much of our technique. Like everything else, flexibility and feeling are developed by practice.

While you're trying to develop this feel, you should also know what you're attempting to do mechanically. As the weight has shifted, the shoulders and hips have turned and the arms have been swung down the target line, the hands will begin to return the clubface to the ball through the unhinging, or uncocking of the wrists. Much has been said and written about this releasing of power and position. But it is still one of the most misunderstood aspects of the golf swing.

Again, like a number of other aspects of the forward swing, releasing the club is a reaction more than an action. Unless you are holding onto the club so tightly or shoving it through from the right side, the swinging action of the arms and the unhinging of the wrists will cause the clubhead to return to the square position immediately before impact. Not AT impact, immediately BEFORE impact. Trying to keep the clubhead square to the line a longer time causes you to leave the clubhead slightly open. That's what we mean when we say you've *blocked* the shot.

Many golfers I've seen think that releasing the club is something actively done with the hands. Instead, it is more of a rotation of the entire left arm as it goes on through the impact area in a firm, swinging action. The left arm does not collapse or bend at impact. The wrist does not break down. The swinging action of the arms does not stop.

Think of it this way: If you're driving your car up to a stop sign you begin to slow down well before coming to the sign. If your swing stops at or even slightly after impact, that means it has started to slow down well before impact. And there goes the whole idea of maximum clubhead speed out the window!

One way to keep yourself swinging well past the ball is to think of the swing as a whole unit of movement that finishes with a feeling of extension and stretch, very much like the feeling you had at the beginning of the backswing. Make the swing wide in that area between the ball and your left knee by stretching and swinging well down the target line. Trying to get that feeling helps you keep your body in position also. You will have less tendency to ''pop up'' by straightening your legs or pulling up your upper body during the swing if you can imagine that long swing out past the golf ball before going up.

Jack Nicklaus tells me he feels like the club is literally chasing the ball out toward the target when he swings this way. That's not a bad feeling for you to have, too.

And one final thing you should experience at the end of every swing: complete balance. Having kept the body and head steady while you're completing the swing, you should find they are in total balance at the end. Falling back to the right or over and around indicate that you haven't let the swing happen but you have forced it to happen with your upper body. A good, completed swing pattern will have a finish with the arms swung up and around, not just up or just around. A finish with the arms still straight and stiff indicates too much tension while one that just goes around shows you that you didn't swing down the target line long enough. A relaxed finish allows the elbows to bend once the arms are high into the finish, with the club going back over the shoulder and back.

A swing in which you've moved the weight totally to the target side and allowed the hips and shoulders to unwind will have a finish with the front of the body, your belt buckle, facing down the target or even left of it and the weight all the way over on the left. The right foot, having completed its pushing off early in the forward swing, will have turned to where it is almost completely upright and vertical. Remember if you don't get a dirty right toe playing golf, you haven't moved totally to the finish.

The weight will have been received by the left foot and transferred to the outer edge of that foot by the finish of the swing. If the weight is only on the left heel, or if the left toe has spun around so that it's facing the target then you didn't make your best swing down the target line. You will have either spun the hips too fast or shoved the right shoulder and the swing path across the target line, forcing body weight back onto the heel.

If we know that the follow-through and finish of a golf swing does not really make the swing itself, then why all this attention to it? Well, as I keep saying, it is the basic fundamental moves and positions, practiced over and over that make you a good golfer. Practicing these positions, even without a club, can help your body learn to recognize what they are and how to get there. And, as we said before, concentrating on getting to the finish helps keep you from stopping everything at the ball.

PUTTING IT ALL TOGETHER

Learning the fundamental moves, then practicing them — that's what makes anyone a good golfer. Not getting yourself tangled up with small details. Not getting yourself bogged down with gimmicks. Learn the simple moves. And learn to do them within your own personal tempo.

Words like tempo, timing, rhythm all convey something different to different people. That's why I don't use them too much. We know Sam Snead's golf swing looks like it's almost in slow motion. But that's Sam's personal speed. Someone like Trevino jumps up and swings at it, BAM-BAM. That's his style. Lopez looks so slow on her backswing you wonder if she'll get there, while if you blink you miss Joanne Carner's whole swing. Each successful player puts together the fundamentals of the golf swing in a repeating way that fits their temperament and personal tempo.

For you to be able to swing repeatedly, you will have to do the same thing. Give each fundamental its place and TIME in your swing and you won't swing too fast. Keep the swing flowing, the power building, and then unwinding. Keep good word pictures in your mind and it will be easier to do. Practice often and it will be easier to do. And keep a good, positive outlook, expecting to make a good swing. Simple fundamentals are the building blocks for that repeating swing with every club. Those blocks are held together by a repeating swing tempo.

CHAPTER FIVE

Short Game Skills

————————

Having spent a great deal of time on the fundamentals of the full golf swing, you may feel like you have the game licked now. The fact of the matter is that you've only started to improve as a player. These next three chapters are where you'll learn how to complement those fundamental skills you already have.

Throughout my career as a teacher and player I've seen many successful players, some of whom were magnificent strikers of the ball. Sam Snead has hit fewer crooked golf shots than anybody I know. Ben Hogan has mechanics as pure as snow. Mickey Wright perfected the swing. Babe Zaharias was as strong a woman hitter as Palmer is a man. But there have been just as many players who were successful because they were masters of the *short* game in golf. And that's where many of those would-be greats coming to the lesson tee need as much work as they do on their swing fundamentals.

Walter Hagen, from 100 yards in and on the green was tremendous. Everything seemed to go in. Part of Bobby Jones' rare skill was that he was a terrific putter. Paul Runyan still is deadly in this area. When he and I were playing, I could usually outdrive him 50 to 100 yards, but he was so marvelous in the short game and bunker play that he won two PGA Championships and was recognized as a truly great player. Horton Smith had it in this area. Sam Snead plays almost flawlessly from bunkers. I could go on and on but you know what I'm saying: the game is more than just

PAUL RUNYAN *is recognized as one of the truly great short game players.*

hitting those long straight shots with woods and irons.

Some of today's organized research has shown just how important the short game is to the good player: 43% of the game is putting, 13% chipping and another 7% short irons.[1] That makes about 63% of the game! Maybe if you are not an experienced and skilled striker of the ball yet, that percentage might be less; but the fact remains that even when you become a great striker of the ball, like the pros, STILL 63% OF YOUR GAME WILL BE THE SHORT GAME! That seems reason enough to put in time on those skilled fundamentals as well.

And if you think that only golfers of the past with great talents were masters of the short game, take a look at today's professionals. Tom Kite, a young man, not unlike Hogan, who has spent a great deal of time and energy on his golf techniques, was reported to have gotten the ball up and down in two from 40 yards away an astounding 85% of the time during the 1984 season. You can bet his fundamentals are sound. And so are those of young Scott Verplank, the 1984 Amateur Champion who became the first amateur in 31 years to win a PGA event when he won the 1985 Western Open. Commentators constantly credit much of his success to his skills in the short game.

You can have good short game skills, too. Let's take a look at how to get started so that you have greater skill and therefore more confidence in this area.

APPROACH SHOTS

Before working on specific techniques let's identify the skills you are trying to improve and develop. Approach shots are as varied as situations on a golf course and the terrain from which they are played. If you find yourself playing one of those wind-swept, flat links courses you will need

---

[1]Dave Pelz Golf Research, Inc., copyright, May, 1983.

to play more low running shots to greens than you will if you're on a course with elevated greens that are well bunkered and protected. That type of course will demand that you play a higher pitch shot that drops vertically without much roll.

Although there is no way you or I can identify all the possible situations and varieties of shots you'll need to play this game well, we can work on some specific fundamentals and there we are again — back to those basics. Your own experience and intellectual assessment of playing conditions will help you learn to adapt and refine these basics to fit the needs of the shot.

One of the things that makes approaching a green difficult, unless it is a full swing with any chosen club, is the many choices you have. Sometimes you may either play it low and running OR high and stopping. Sometimes you need to go 60 yards and you're not sure how far or fast to swing the club to make the ball go 60 yards. Then your next approach shot is only 57 yards and you're not sure how to hit it differently from the way you hit it for 60 yards. There are just more decisions to be made. So one of the fundamentals you'll need to have is some basic guidelines.

Ben Hogan was once quoted as having said he'd rather play a pitch shot because, as long as he had the ball in the air, he felt he could control it. Once it started rolling across a green as in a low running chip shot, he felt Mother Nature was more in control. But most of us who play this game don't have Hogan's finesse with our swings. Mother Nature may not be that bad a risk! The rule of thumb or guideline I would give you is this: When there is enough green to roll the ball, then chip it. And we know that the majority of our approach shots have some green to work with. Any time there is more green between yourself and the flagstick than there is fairway or rough between yourself and the green, then chipping is a must.

So that's your first guideline, chip it if possible. The second one is equally simple: Try to control the distance you hit the ball with the simplest modifications possible. That is, don't try to do all sorts of fancy, risky stuff with the ball when it's not necessary at all.

Most approach shots, once you've decided whether to pitch or chip, demand only that you choose the correct club and make a short swing. Once again I stress it IS simple, but it is NOT easy unless you spend your time practicing and getting comfortable with the idea.

The easiest way to control the distance a ball goes is to choose a shorter and more lofted club. But when you get to the gray area of approach shots where you are not making a full swing with any club, you need to know yourself, your preferences and your abilities.

We'll discuss specific club selections when we talk about pitch shots and chip shots individually, but for now let's identify the guideline for controlling distance with all clubs. Basically you control distance by controlling how far back you swing and how fast you accelerate through the ball. You know that already from the earlier fundamentals. The problem comes when you don't commit yourself to one of these.

If you follow the guideline of making the simplest modification possible, you will learn to control the length of your backswing while maintaining a constant swing tempo. As you get more advanced in your shot-making skills, you will recognize opportunities where a number of modifications will give you shots with a variety of characteristics, but for the basic approach shot learn how far the ball will go with a variety of short swings. Establish some checkpoints for yourself.

Many people visualize their swings as following the numbers on a clockface. The backswing may go to the number nine, or 9 o'clock, and the follow-through to 3 o'clock; or backswing to 8 and follow-through to 4, etc. Practicing will tell you the distance each combination gives you, but remember the importance of the follow-through. You do not want to make a 9 o'clock to 6 o'clock swing, or anything to stop at six, for that matter. It will never be consistent.

If you concentrate on finishing on the other side of the "clock" you can continue the swing at an accelerating but constant speed. Many golfers get anxious or careless with short approach shorts and lose their repeating natural tempo. Remember that no matter how short the swing is, it is a full swinging pattern, not a chop. And it should not be faster than your normal full swing nor so slow that you lose acceleration.

The third general guideline for all approach shots is to use visualization in your planning. Unless you can see what you want to have happen, you have very little chance of making it happen. Unless you have planned totally, it will be hard to commit yourself to action. And unless you can have confidence in your plan, it will be impossible to play aggressively in your short game.

An old golf adage says, "Winners see what they want to have happen while losers see what they are afraid will happen." That should be your guideline for visualization in the short game. Any time you plan an approach shot, you should be able to pinpoint in your mind's eye what the flight of the ball will look like, where the ball will land, and how far it will roll after landing. Only then can you have a target area for landing the ball.

As you can tell following these guidelines is a total process, not so much a 1-2-3 step-by-step plan. It's hard to choose whether to chip or pitch without first visualizing your shot results. It's impossible to know how far back to swing the club unless you know where you want to land the ball. All three guidelines are interconnected. And all three go into making you a thinking golfer. Learning to be a thinking golfer is as important as learning to hit your wedge.

Following general guidelines for approaching the green help you organize your thinking about this part of the game. But it does not take the place of having good fundamental skills in pitching and chipping, nor does it account for all the differences you may face in different lies, on different grasses and under different playing conditions. Let's look first at the skills you need to play the different approach shots.

CHIP SHOT

The fundamental skills of chipping are simply variations of those used in the full swing. A good grip, correct aim, and efficient set-up are necessary. The grip should be positioned lower on the club, sometimes almost onto the metal portion of the shaft. The reason for this is that it will give you greater control over the shot. And, of course, the distance requirement for a chip shot is less than for a full swing, so you will not need the full length of the club shaft. The ball and swing should be aimed at the spot you expect to land the ball. Remember, you will have a great deal of roll after a chip shot lands, but you are looking at the landing area as your point of aim.

The set-up will have the feet closer together and closer to the ball than on a full swing. The shorter the shot (and therefore the swing), the closer the feet to each other and to the ball, because you will position your hands lower on the club for shorter shots. Most people prefer to open the stance slightly when setting up to chip. That position makes it easier to keep the swing path on line with the target and makes it easier to "feel" the shot.

Your head must remain absolutely steady for this little golf swing. You're not trying to create a lot of power here, just finesse. Practice hitting chip shots with your weight totally on your left foot, your right toes barely touching the ground. That drill will allow you to feel how steady you must be. This will also help you feel the position of a set-up with the majority of the body weight on the target, or left side.

Shifting weight is not needed in chipping. Staying on the target side

CHIP SHOTS *require some variation from the full swing.*

makes it easier to swing through the ball, contacting it right before the bottom of the swing arc, just like your full iron swing. But just because you set up with the weight left, don't set up stiff and tight. Keep a lively feeling in the knees and legs.

The arms and shoulders also must feel alive, without unnecessary tension. Unless they are relaxed enough to swing freely through the ball, the body will be more likely to move around during the swing. Or, if you're tense over the ball, the swing may not come off as a swing at all, but as a chop or hit.

A final checkpoint for getting ready to chip the ball is to make sure you have your hands ever so slightly ahead of the golf ball. This will help you keep the hands and forearms leading the clubhead through the ball. If the clubhead were to pass the arms and hands you would get a weak, scooped shot or a topped shot that would not yield planned results. This slight forward press position also keeps the ball flight low.

The swing for a chip shot will be primarily along the target line. With your slightly open stance you must take great care to keep the swing going toward the target and not along your feet. Because most chip shots are not very long, 20-40 yards at the most, the swing can stay really close to the target line. Your swing thought should be centered around making a smooth, complete swing along the line to the target.

The swing arc will be fairly shallow. Try to keep the wrists quiet during a chip shot. If it is a particularly long shot in which the club has to travel through a longer backswing with the hands going back to 9 o'clock, then some wrist cock will occur as the right elbow hinges slightly. But for a short chip in which the hands go back to only 7 or 8 o'clock at most, the hands and wrists are firm. The arms and shoulders swing the club back and forth through the ball with a swing that keeps the clubhead near the ground at all times.

That's about all there is to making a chip shot swing. But there is one other consideration in chipping, club selection. Many fine golfers prefer to choose one club for the majority of their chip shots, perhaps an 8-iron. Others like to choose a club based on the demands of the situation. By gripping down on the club and making a short swing you can get the same overall distance from a variety of irons. The difference will be in the ratio of ball flight to roll.

If you're right off the edge of the green and the flagstick is near the opposite edge of the green, a 6-iron might be your choice. With this club you may expect about one-third of the total distance to be ball flight and the remainder to be roll. The same situation with the flagstick only 15 feet onto the green would call for a more lofted club, perhaps an 8-iron. With this club about two-thirds of the total distance would be in ball flight and only one-third roll.

Spending some time learning how you hit chip shots with different irons is the only way you can decide your preferences for club selection. Once you have a good idea of both the distances you hit the ball and the ratio of ball flight to roll, you can then take these fundamentals to the course. But to be completely skilled at approach shots you should also know the fundamentals of a pitch shot.

PITCH SHOT

Many fundamentals of the pitch are very similar to those of the chip. The grip is still your basic good grip which will be positioned lower on the club for shorter shots. Your aim will be toward the landing spot you have chosen on the green. And your set-up will be slightly open stance with the feet closer together than for a full swing. As in the chip shot, the feet may be much closer together for very short shots.

Because of the precision required in this shot the head again must remain very steady. But unlike the chip shot, the weight may shift slight-ly, and naturally, during the pitch. This shifting will be more obvious with

PITCH SHOTS *call for precision and a steady head.*

the longer swing, and will not happen so much in the very short shot.

Arms and shoulders must be relaxed, ready to swing. Wrists will be more active in the pitch. The major difference between the pitch and the chip is the higher ball flight of the pitch which, in turn, results in less roll. One way that higher ball flight is attained is simply to use the more lofted clubs like the 9-iron and the wedges.

But the swing itself is a more V-shaped swing pattern than the chip. Swinging the arms back while allowing the right elbow to hinge and the wrists to cock creates a more vertical backswing for the pitch swing. Returning the club through the ball by swinging the arms toward the target will then bring the swing into the ball more steeply. Referring to our earlier theories of ball flight you can see that that sharper angle of attack will cause the ball to fly higher.

As in the chip shot, the swing should be started from a position with the hands slightly ahead of the ball to insure that first contact on the downswing will be the ball and not the ground behind it. If you want to be a good pitch shot player you must always keep the swing accelerating through the ball on to a high finish. As Patty Berg says, ''Swing high to watch it fly!''

Again I want to caution you about the urge to scoop up the ball. If you keep your backswing compact and your tempo smooth you will swing through. If you get long and floppy on the backswing you risk decelerating your forward swing and/or scooping up the ball. Even though you want to hit the ball high into the air, you must strike the ball slightly before the bottom of your swing arc.

Club selection in pitching is less of a problem than in chipping but again you need to get out and practice with your highly lofted clubs. Some players now carry as many as three different wedges to have a variety of pitching clubs to choose from. Whatever clubs you have in your bag, make sure you have a good idea of what to do with each of them.

OTHER FACTORS TO CONSIDER

Although you can never identify all the situations you will face in making approach shots, there are one or two that bear mentioning. Deciding how far you personally can hit a certain approach shot is only part of knowing how to play it. You have to also be able to determine the effect of other factors.

You should evaluate the lie of the ball. A ball sitting down in tall grass will roll more after it hits the green than a ball sitting cleanly on short grass. That's what the pros call a "flyer." The grass gets between the clubface and the ball and prevents backspin that helps stop the ball.

A ball sitting on a slope will behave differently from a ball sitting on level ground. If the ball's on an uphill slope the shot will go higher, therefore shorter, and stop sooner after hitting. On a downhill, the ball will fly lower and roll more.

A soft green will absorb a pitch shot, making it bite and stop sooner than will a hard green. Coarse green grasses such as Bermuda will cause the ball to stop quicker than will fine grasses such as bent, fescue, and bluegrass.

A strong wind behind you will not only cause the ball to fly further, it will also add to the roll. A head wind will provide the opposite effect. Cross winds will especially affect high pitch shots.

All of these additional considerations bring me back to the fact that none of us can escape. You have to go out and play the game and practice your skills to be able to cope with everything you find during a round of golf. It is a game in which the mental challenges keep popping up as fast as the physical ones.

Speaking of these mental challenges reminds me of the final thought for you to keep in mind when playing an approach shot. So much of this part of the game is developing feel for the shot. Allowing the knowledge you have to help you choose the exact shot and exact swing necessary to do the job. To make the very best use of that knowledge you must trust your feel and muscle memory. Even professionals take one or more practice swings before hitting an approach shot. I suggest that you learn to do the same.

Your full swing may not need a dry run rehearsal before each shot, but this small, partial swing does. Look at the target and take a swing letting your eyes help you ''feel'' the distance. You don't have to consciously know exactly what is happening. Just try to feel the total swing pattern you're expecting to make. Then when you step up ready for the shot, try to make the swing feel the same. That habit of taking a practice swing will be one more way to build a repeating short game.

PUTTING

If there is any part of this game in which you can be individual, it is in the area of putting. And if there is any area in which you can shine, no matter what your strength, age, coordination, or whatever may inhibit your building excellent skills in other areas, it is on the green. Anyone who takes the time to learn the fundamentals and practices them enough to gain confidence can be an excellent putter.

And if you are an excellent putter, that certainly makes it easier to play other shots. Knowing you can two-putt from anywhere on the green doesn't put as much pressure on your short game or your full swings to the green as would exist if you HAVE to put it close. In fact, if you find you have a lot of pressure on all your shots, it could be traced right back to the lack of confidence in putting.

How can you gain confidence in this aspect? In putting, as well as other areas of the game ''confidence comes from competence.'' And competence comes from basic fundamentals and hard work on them. Nothing new.

What is new in putting is the necessity for reading the green. Reading greens successfully is one of the most difficult skills to describe as well as to master. Basically, it is the skill of evaluating the slope of the surface along which the putt will roll, the speed at which the ball will roll, and the other characteristics of the surface such as grain, length of grass, smoothness or roughness of grass, and a variety of other subtle potential effects on the planned putt.

Learning to read greens is just like learning the feel of a correct grip or the distance you swing the club back for a 20-yard chip. It takes a lot of practice. And it takes being "tuned in" to what you are practicing. Making mental notes of how something looks and how the ball behaves so that the next time you observe a similar putt you have something to fall back on.

A drill in which you put four golf balls around a practice hole that is located on a slope can help you learn about breaks. Place balls north, east, south and west around the hole the same distance away. Putt each ball in, observing each different break. Try to get three or more balls in from each of the four points as a challenge to yourself.

Place tees on a practice green at various distances and practice hitting a ball to each of those distances to learn the speed of the green. Then try to hit a putt one-half the distance, then one-quarter the distance. Call your shot before making it. Compete with yourself or a playing partner.

But even if you master the art of reading greens successfully you will not be a great putter if you cannot count on your putting skills to be consistent. To make them repeatable and confidence-inspiring, you only have to control two factors, distance and direction. Now, before you chuckle at the obvious statement, remember that it hasn't been too long that golf greens have been totally manicured so that the roll of putts would be predictable. Bobby Jones' famous Calamity Jane putter had a two-degree loft to it. When he had a long putt, he'd lay it back a little and sort of lob it up toward the hole. When it was a short putt, he'd forward press his

BOBBY JONES' *putting skills were among his finest attributes as a player.*

hands and roll the ball in. However he made it work, Jones was indeed one of the best putters I've ever seen.

To become a terrific putter yourself you need a balanced, comfortable stance and set-up. Whatever position you choose you should have the body weight located over the ball position. And you should bend enough at the waist to have your eyes over the ball or on the target line and slightly behind the ball. You never want to get your eyes outside your target line. It will interfere with your ability to strike the ball consistently along that line.

The body weight must remain absolutely still with no shift and no movement of the head until well after the ball is struck. I have seen even professional golfers move their heads and upper bodies to follow the ball, only to find that they moved while they were striking the ball and what they were seeing was not a good putt. Develop the habit of waiting to listen for a putt to drop or simply swiveling your head, not raising up, to see the putt go on its way.

Hold the club in a comfortable, light grip of your preference. A number of golfers use the reverse overlapping grip in which the little finger of the right hand is on the club and the forefinger of the left overlaps it. Others use a cross-handed grip in which the left hand is on the club lower down the grip than is the right hand. This type of grip assists some golfers in keeping the wrists quiet and firm throughout the stroke. Nearly all putting grips have the thumbs pointing down the grip.

Elbows should be fairly close to the body and will usually be slightly bent because of the body's being bent over at the waist. U.S. Open Champion Andy North uses a slightly different arm position. He keeps the arms straight, much like the set-up for a chip shot.

Whatever position is chosen for the elbows, nearly every successful professional player uses an arm swing method with little or no wrist involvement. Bobby Jones said the essence of putting was to simply keep the back of the left hand toward the target at all times. This effectively keeps the arms and shoulders moving the club back and forth along the line with the clubface square.

Going back to our earlier assessment of what controls direction, you know that the primary determinants of direction are the path along which you swing the club and the position of the clubface when it strikes the ball. These are the two factors you must control in your putting to hit the ball straight toward your target.

Some of the latest research shows us a surprising result: It's more important that you have the clubface square than that you be swinging on a straight path. Don't get me wrong, doing either incorrectly will send the ball off line. It's just that I see a lot of players working on their swing path and not paying much attention to the squareness of the clubface.

Practicing a putting stroke can be done most anywhere. Put down two other clubs or two yardsticks or anything to form a tunnel in which you can swing your putter to really show you how straight your club path is. Checking clubface position is a little more difficult. One easy way is to place two golf balls side by side. Strike both of them with your putter. They will roll approximately the same distance if the putter head is square to the line. If the one closer to your feet goes further you know the heel of your club got to the balls before the toe; if the other goes further you know the toe got there first. Practice until both balls leave the clubface together.

Hitting the ball on the sweet spot of your putter will also affect the direction and distance the ball will go. Identify the sweet spot by tapping your putter with a quarter or even a golf ball every few milimeters along its face while holding it lightly by the grip end. When you tap it off the sweet spot, the putter will wiggle. When you tap it on the sweet spot, it will swing like a pendulum. If your putter does not have a marking on the top of the blade to indicate the position of the sweet spot you might put one there with a permanent substance like paint. That will provide you with one more visual cue to assist you in putting.

Distance for many players provides a greater challenge than direction. Who can forget the sight of the young contender a few years ago in the British Open sadly and helplessly watching his putt not only go past the hole but off the green into a gaping pit bunker. While most of your distance "misses" may not be that deadly, I'm sure you could take a few strokes off your game by getting the ball closer to the hole more often on approach putts.

In addition to hitting the ball consistently on the sweet spot, the major fundamentals affecting distance are the length of the swing and the speed of the swing. As you notice these are exactly the same ones that affect the distance for any shot. Of course, you can never get away from having to judge the rolling speed of the ball, too; but once having made that decision, you want to have a consistent stroke to give you the desired distance.

Long putts, and by that I mean those over eight feet, should be played so as to never have to worry about the next time. Sounds simple enough, but everybody occasionally has those mental lapses that produces a second putt longer than the first! To minimize that possibility you need to learn first how to control the tempo of the putting stroke. Even with less than perfect mechanics you still have a chance to "miss it close," if you have a predictable tempo to your stroke. Sally Little, considered one of the best putters on the LPGA Tour, said it was because she could control the tempo of her stroke. Putting, like every other shot in golf, must be an accelerating swing. Note the word SWING. Putting is a small, rhythmic swinging of the club. Back and through. Just like a drive, only in a smaller space.

Changing the tempo, rushing the forward swing, jerking the club back, failing to accelerate, stopping at the ball . . . all of these swing errors negatively affect a putt just like a full swing. Tempo is so important that it is a good cue for the actual swing execution. Thinking ''1-2'' or ''back-through'' can often keep your swing in rhythm during a pressure putt.

One error that sometimes make it difficult to keep an even paced putting tempo that accelerates through the ball is too long a backswing. If you swing the putter back so far that you know you'll hit the ball well past your target, then you tend to stop at the ball or slow down coming into it. Practice keeping a compact, but not jerky, backswing.

Just as with your short approach shots, long putts require visualization and a practice swing. If you make that practice swing while looking at the hole you may find that helps your muscles ''feel'' the right distance through which to swing. First of all, aim the ball from behind as with any shot. Visualize the entire roll of the ball. See the line. Again you may find it helpful to use an intermediate target on the line near the ball. Take your set-up position relative to the target line. Now, for practice, try hitting a few long putts while looking at the hole. Never look down at the ball, always at the hole. You'll find you're pretty successful in getting that ball close to the hole and I bet you'll very seldom if ever wind up short. Use that technique of looking at the hole for your *practice* swing. Make it part of your pre-shot routine. And then simply try to make your actual putting stroke FEEL like your practice one. Don't analyze it while you're putting. Think a tempo thought and try to make it feel like the practice swing.

One more thing about those long putts. Remember, I said that anything over eight feet I would count as a long putt. The reason I chose that distance is that is the distance where the putting robot begins to miss about 50% of its putts. Don't expect to miss them there, but accept it if you do. Jane Blalock says that she knows that every putt CAN go in, but she doesn't *expect* every putt TO go in.

In adopting a realistic outlook like that you should plan to have your long putts stop in a target area surrounding the hole. How big that target is depends upon how good you are with short putts. If you sink most every putt from four feet in, then your target area can be eight feet wide, four feet on all sides of the hole. But if you're confident only from two feet, then your target can only be four feet wide. That alone should show you how important it is to practice those short ones so the long ones are easier. So for your longer putts choose a target area, not just the hole itself.

Whether you are a bold putter who charges the hole or a lag putter preferring to leave the ball safe and short is somewhat related to your playing personality. And sometimes it will reflect good playing strategy. But another item from research gives us a clue as to which is more efficient. A putt that is hit firmly so as to go slightly past the hole, if it does not go in, will have a better chance of holding the line and of not being affected by irregularities on the green. That says it pretty clearly. Tom Watson, who is noted for his bold putting style, adds his comment in favor of a well struck putt: ''If it goes by the hole I just pay close attention to how it broke and that helps me plan my putt coming back!''

That ''coming back'' putt or any other short putt provides you the chance to make that final recovery or to miss it forever. If you think about it, you can make up any missed shot on a hole EXCEPT that lost short putt. Missing a three-foot putt costs as much as whiffing your drive!

Repeatability of your stroke, smooth controlled tempo, absolutely steady body position . . . these are the things that give you confidence in short putts. Careful planning of aim and execution can't be overlooked. And practice, practice, and more practice. Use your intermediate target spot and send that ball right over it toward your target. Visualize the entire roll of the ball just as you would a long putt. See the line it will roll along vividly and totally. Keep a consistent routine. Commit yourself to your chosen action. Think a basic tempo cue and swing. It's as easy as that once you've practiced and developed confidence in your stroke.

SUMMARY

Putting, chipping and pitching are all skills that everyone can master. Without the strength of a Jack Nicklaus or a Patty Sheehan, without the swing arc of a Tom Weiskopf or a Beth Daniel, without the talent of a Sam Snead or Mickey Wright you can still learn these skills. And considering how much of the game rests on them, you can definitely learn to be a better golfer by mastering them. They are not so exciting as hitting drives 200 yards straight down the middle. But remember all the times you may have hit that 200 yard drive only to take numerous strokes around and/or on the green. And remember the thrill of chipping the ball up close enough for a tap in to save par. Which is more important in the long run?

CHAPTER SIX
Trouble Shots

I have always thought that ''trouble shots'' was the wrong term to use for these skills. Actually what you're learning are those shots that get you OUT OF trouble, so I prefer to think of them as recovery skills. Bobby Jones once said what everyone who plays the game knows, ''You can't keep from getting into trouble in golf so you'd better learn how to get out of it!''

Just like approach shots, you'll never know all the possible combinations of challenges a golf course can throw at you. And just when you think you have your basic fundamentals mastered, you'll hit a ball off the face of the earth. All that is left to do at that time is, as Arnold Palmer once said, ''Go find it and hit it again.''

Many times, your measure as a thinking golfer is in how you handle trouble. The player who coolly assesses the problem and goes about solving it, based on a good grasp of both ball flight laws and his own skills, will be able to play this game. The player who allows his reactions to adversity to cloud his thinking and planning, or who hasn't taken the time to learn basic skills of recovery, will always have a hard time posting low numbers consistently.

But just like every other skill in golf, playing the ball from unusual circumstances takes practice. Trying to pull off any shot that you've never practiced is risky; trying to do it under the pressure of getting out of trouble is almost impossible.

CHAPTER SIX

Let's look at some of those shots you can practice. As I said before you're never going to know all the possible circumstances. But that's where your brain comes in again, learning to adapt some basic recovery shot to a specific situation. Having confidence in the fundamental skill gives you a chance to make a decent recovery that won't cost you strokes.

HITTING FROM UNUSUAL LIES

If you're a good course manager, that is, you play the game intelligently, you'll always assess the lie of the ball first. If you can't get it out of where it is, there's not much need to worry about where it's going! Three different kinds of lies provide trouble for many golfers: bare or tight lie; heavy or long grass lie; a lie in a divot hole.

BARE OR TIGHT LIE

Often your definition of a tight lie depends upon what part of the country you're from. Golfers used to hitting off the matted low running grasses of the South may feel secure hitting off the sidewalk, while players at home on the longer, more upright blades up North feel insecure unless the ball is sitting down in the grass. But everyone has to notice those times that the ball is sitting on ''hardpan,'' or hard, dry turf or earth.

Whatever creates anxiety for you, there are some simple rules for hitting off a tight lie. First of all remember that you must strike the ball on the downswing to get it airborne from a tight lie. To help yourself do that, move the ball back in your stance about an inch. Keep your hands in the position they would be in if the ball were not moved back, that is, ahead of the ball. Now, by swinging down and forward with the wrists firm and the left side leading you can be sure you will hit the ball before the ground. And it will make it harder to try to scoop or sweep the ball off the surface, two deadly errors from this kind of lie.

Practice this shot with a variety of clubs, always moving the ball back

THIS DRILL, *in which you hit balls from a board, will give you confidence in playing shots from tight lies.*

slightly from its normal position for the club you're using. And even with fairway woods, go ahead and swing in a more vertical downswing pattern. Look for a bare spot on your practice range. Or if you cannot find one, make your own practice situation for this shot. Imbed a small piece of soft wood, such as a length of 2''x4'' in the ground on your target line. Dent the surface with the heel of your club so that the ball will sit on it. CAUTION: Only use the end of the board nearer the target so that a swing that hits behind the ball will not hit behind the board but rather on it. Start with short, partial swings with a middle iron until you have confidence in your ability to hit the ball cleanly from the surface of the wood. Move to full swings with all clubs. Practicing this drill from time to time makes even the barest lie look good.

HEAVY OR LONG GRASS

A ball sitting in heavy rough can pose one of two problems. If it is well down into the grass, there is the problem of getting it out. If it is sitting up on top of it, there is the problem of literally swinging the club under the ball not through it.

Playing a ball sitting down in thick heavy grass demands a swing that is upright and a club that is lofted. Swinging the club in a sweeping shallow arc allows the grass to grab the hosel of the club, turning the clubface to a closed position before it gets to the ball. Because that position makes the ball go low and left, that type of swing is particularly ineffective with a long iron. Fairway woods can be used if the grass is not too long.

To have the best chance possible to get out of this type of lie, make the following adjustments for your shot: choose the club most likely to get you out and close to the hole, but get out first; play the ball back a little in your stance; open the clubface slightly at address to compensate for the closing action of the grass on the hosel; keep a firm, strong grip on the club; swing the club back in an upright pattern making a full shoulder turn, then down with a steep angle of attack to minimize the amount of time the club's in the grass; keep the left side leading the swing to its finish.

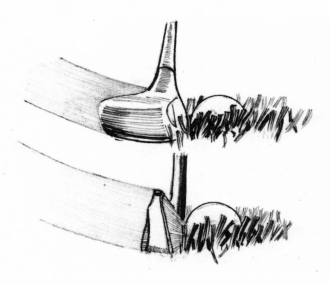

PLAYING A SHOT *from long rough demands a firm grip and a steep angle of attack to cut through the grass.*

Two other factors for consideration in hitting this kind of shot have to do with landing area and aiming. In choosing your landing area remember that a ball hit from long grass will have less backspin than a ball hit from the fairway. This lack of backspin will cause the ball to fly lower and also run longer once it hits the ground. But before you start dropping down one or two clubs, also consider the resistance your swing will encounter by the grass. A strong swinging motion will be necessary to gain the full distance of the club you choose. Only practice will show you the distance you can expect from each of your clubs in this type of lie.

To further compensate for the closing of the clubface you may choose to aim slightly right of your desired target when playing out of this situation. For golfers who do not have as much upper body and hand strength, particularly women and seniors, this is a very important modification. But remember one guideline that should control all your aiming techniques. Ben Hogan said it best when he said to always aim at the "mowed stuff." In order words, don't try to con your body into aiming at more trouble with the idea it will compensate. You're likely to find that your body won't follow orders and you'll end up further into the trouble you're trying to avoid. So don't aim yourself so far right that you'll go back into the rough you're trying to escape. Aim to the right side of the fairway instead.

If the ball is sitting up on top of the heavy grass, like it does in Bermuda rough then your problem is a little different. Unless you examine the lie carefully you may find yourself having executed a perfect swing with some not-so-perfect results. If you note that the grass is deep underneath the ball, then choose a less lofted club, expecting the ball to be struck higher on the clubface as the club passes through the grass. A second modifiction is at address. Hold the club behind the ball, not soled in the grass. Swing with a sweeping, strong motion going well through the ball, not so much down on it as when it was sitting down in the grass. Again you will have a better chance to strike the ball first by moving it slightly back in your stance at address.

PLAYING A BALL *which is resting on top of heavy, coarse grass demands more of a sweeping motion.*

FROM A DIVOT

Hitting from a long, shallow divot hole is very similar to hitting from a bare or tight lie. The most important thing in hitting this shot is also a factor in any recovery shot. Make sure you do not let yourself get so upset at being IN trouble that you can't get OUT OF trouble. An upright swing which contacts the ball first with a downward arc is again the method of recovery you should use. One thing that sometimes happens in getting out of a divot is the heel of the club hits first, messing up the shot. Set up with the heel of your club slightly raised off the ground to insure that you'll swing through the ball without bouncing into it. With this unusual lie you'll also need to keep your hands slightly ahead to make sure you do not scoop the ball.

This is one of the easiest shots to play on your practice range. Every range has divot holes. Put a few balls into them and play them out with different clubs. You'll soon discover your abilities and limitations with this shot. Then you can use it successfully in play.

Unusual lies are not the only challenges presented during the play of a round. Other differences found in the terrain of a golf course present challenges as well.

PLAYING THE TOPOGRAPHY OF THE COURSE

At many golf courses playing the ball from an uneven or non-level lie is not a matter of being in trouble so much as it is the nature of a particular course! Even golfers whose home courses have a variety of uphill, downhill, and sidehill lies sometimes don't know how to play those kinds of shots consistently. Anyone can learn the basic modifications necessary. Practice gives you confidence in making them.

UPHILL AND DOWNHILL LIES

Playing a ball up a slope or down it can be a simple shot if you have confidence in what to do. The problem I see is that many golfers don't spend enough time evaluating the ball position and ignore slight variations in lie. First of all, LOOK at your ball and if there is a slight up or down ground slant under it, make a SLIGHT adjustment.

The basic modification for either up or down hill shots is to move the ball in your stance. It has a simple reason: the bottom of the arc will not touch the ground in the same way it does when the ground is level. The actual placement of the ball can be remembered if you simple PLAY THE BALL NEARER THE HIGH FOOT. How much nearer will depend upon how steep the slope. Take a practice swing to show yourself where it should be. Wherever your club starts its divot is the bottom of the arc. Your ball should be placed just barely back of that so that you'll contact it on the downswing. Taking a practice swing shows you this spot.

Although ball positioning is the major modification for these two shots, there are a couple of other important ones. To allow your swing to follow the contour of the slope and not either dig into it or totally miss it, align your shoulders with the slope. By that I mean if you're hitting uphill then leave the right shoulder slightly lower than the left. If you're hitting downhill, allow the right shoulder to come up slightly so that the shoulder line more closely follows the line of the hill. And, secondly, lean your body weight into the hill just like you would in skiing. Use your legs and and feet to hold the body against the power of the swing. Keep your weight to the inside of both feet to prevent the head and shoulders from moving outside your base of support. Just as in the full swing, balance is the key to a successful shot.

To maintain that balance you may have to shorten your swing pattern somewhat and not swing at top speed. Moderation is always a good thought when playing from any unusual or trouble situation. You may find, too, that you have to use a different club from what you'd use on level ground. Hitting a ball off an upslope will give you a shorter, higher shot, while hitting it from a downhill lie will give you a lower, longer ball flight. Whichever club you choose, make sure that you complete your swing along the slope for as long as possible to insure sound contact with the clubhead.

SIDEHILL LIES

Sidehill lies are those in which you find the ball somewhat below or somewhat above your feet at address. The one where the ball's above your feet is generally accepted to be the easier of the two, but both can be played successfully if you know the modifications and practice them.

When the ball is higher up the slope than where you are standing, your swing will be flatter. This makes sense if you can imagine a steep slope where the ball is almost at your knee level; you'd be making almost a baseball swing at it! If you have a very steep slope from which to play the ball, then you'd better first drop down to a fairly short club for control. If the slope is more gradual, you may use the same club you'd hit if it were a level lie. To hit the ball first you should place it more or less in the center of your stance. You will stand a bit more upright and your body weight should lean into the hill. The feeling will be one of the knees and the balls of the feet pressing toward the hill. You need to make sure that you swing along the target line for as long as possible with this shot. Otherwise, you'll risk pulling the ball left and/or falling back away from the target line (down the hill) during the forward swing. Again, a three-quarter length swing as opposed to a full, attacking swing provides more balance and control for this type of shot.

The shot with the ball below your feet is one of the most challenging in golf. In fact, it is one of the most difficult to execute correctly while keeping your balance. That should tell you it's one you need to practice often, and not just when you need to make it perfectly to save par and win a bet!

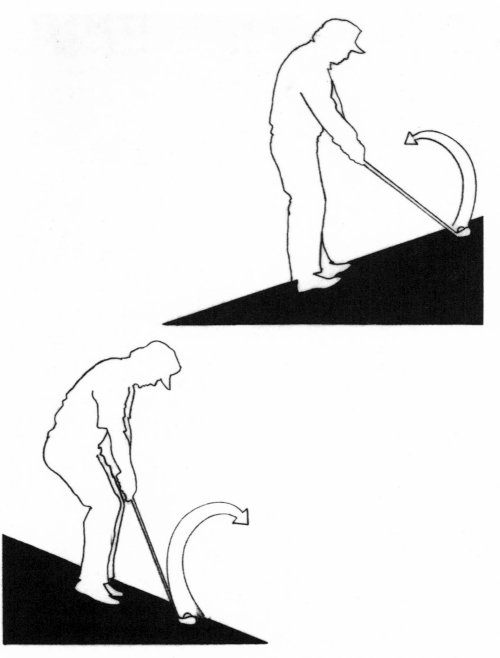

SHOTS FROM *uphill, downhill and sidehill require different address and swing patterns.*

Again, you have to lean into the hill to stabilize yourself. It should feel like a rod has gone down your back to brace you on the hillside. That means you keep your good address position with the shoulders out over the swing line and the weight still between the balls and heels of the feet. But you will feel a little more weight to the instep side of the heels, particularly if it's a steep hill. Your knees may be a little more bent, too.

The ball will be in the center of the stance and you may have to go to a longer club if the ball is well below your feet. Another reason for going to a longer club is that in making this shot it's pretty near impossible to take a full swing and keep your balance. Now, if it's only a small difference in the slope with the ball only an inch or so below your feet, you may hardly make any adjustment at all. But if the hill is steep you will risk losing your balance down the hill and falling forward across your target line if you make a great big full shoulder turn. A smooth turn, trying to make your best three-quarter length swing, is the best bet. And just like the last shot, you have to stretch down along the target line through impact to keep the ball flying toward your target. If the hill is really steep, you may even have to aim a bit to the left to allow for some natural slicing that may occur when the impact is not totally square. But again, be careful not to fall forward during your forward swing. That will force your upper body outside the swing line causing you to pull the ball. If you've already aimed to the left you could be in even more trouble.

As I said before, it's a tricky shot to master, but most golfers are faced with it at one time or another. Ignoring it on the practice range will not keep it from popping up in playing situations! Another shot that pops up in almost every round of golf is one from a sand bunker. We could do a whole book about that area of our games!

SAND PLAY
Sam Snead is one of the truly great bunker players in the game of

golf. And although he is certainly one of the most talented golfers who ever lived, he says he got to be a good bunker player the same way you can; he practiced. It seems when he was growing up he got bored hitting to greens so to work on his aiming abilities he started trying to hit various sand traps on the course he played. All that hitting out of those traps taught him a lot about sand and gave him the confidence to play from it.

You may get your share of sand traps without having to aim at them, but the fact remains that you need the confidence that sound fundamentals and practice will bring you. With the differences in texture of sand, the differences in kinds of bunkers and the differences in course design from place to place, you can expect to encounter a number of different kinds of sand shots in your golfing career. But let's look at the fundamentals for playing from a fairway bunker and from a greenside bunker.

FAIRWAY BUNKER SHOTS

Nowhere do you need to pay close attention to the lie of the ball and the obstacles, namely the edge of the bunker, more than when you're in a fairway trap. Your first objective must be to get out of the sand. If it takes a sand wedge to do that, then use it. I see more players look first at the distance to the green, choose the club to carry it, and then drill the ball right into the edge of the trap or hit so far behind the ball that they never get it airborne! They, and you, must first choose a club that will get the ball over the edge of the bunker and AS FAR AS POSSIBLE down the fairway toward the hole.

If you're in fairly firm sand with the ball sitting up, there is not much of a lip to the bunker, and you can stand on a level surface, then you can hit with almost any club in your bag. The fairway woods with ridges on the bottom work great in this type of situation. But in anything less than these perfect conditions, you'd better choose a club which not only will get you over the lip but which you can also swing with control.

The fundamental modifications for playing a shot from a fairway bunker are these: Move the ball back slightly in your stance to make sure you'll hit the ball first. Keep your hands ahead of the ball. (Remember this will make the ball fly out a little lower than your normal shot with the same club, keep that in mind in planning the shot.) Grip down on the club slightly and go ahead and dig into the sand with your feet for a firm base from which to swing. Make a good, smooth swing, keeping the body balanced throughout. The tendency is to rush the swing because of anxiety. Swinging fast does not allow the full shoulder turn to take place, and it will also cause you to lose your balance. Losing your balance can cause you to hit behind the ball or top it. Either one can leave you with the ball still in the trap. Keep your eyes glued on the ball throughout the swing to stay steady with the head behind the ball. Keep a smooth tempo throughout the swing. You'll have a good chance to get out of the bunker and back on your way toward the green.

TO BE CONSISTENT *in sand play, don't hurry your shots.*

GREENSIDE BUNKER SHOTS

If you don't have a good sand wedge, playing from a greenside bunker is difficult. Get yourself a sand wedge you have confidence in and that is suited to your play and the bunkers on your course. Your golf professional will help you pick one that will work. Unless you have confidence in your equipment and your swing, sand can be more trouble that anyone needs.

Plan your bunker shot based on your abilities. By that I mean to look at making a successful shot as a four-step process. First, you want to ALWAYS get out of the sand. Once you're confident that you can always get out, then try to ALWAYS get on the green. Once you can do that nearly every time, then try to ALWAYS get close the the flagstick. And finally, if you get to be really perfect you can try to ALWAYS go in the hole. I doubt even touring pros try that one! If you're playing a round and you begin to lose confidence, then drop back one objective. Instead of trying to get it close, try to get on the green. That's the realistic way of handling the pressures of a match. Once you're off the course get back to your lessons and practice to regain the confidence you once had.

No matter the objective of your swing, the fundamentals are the same for greenside bunker play. First of all, evaluate the total situation before playing the shot. That means check out the lie of your ball, the distance you have to travel, the height of the lip, the distance between the ball and the lip, the consistency of the sand (you can sort of feel this with your feet while setting up to the ball), the amount of green you have to work with, the slope of the green, and anything else that will influence the ball once it hits the green.

This is another area where I see many players blow the chance for a good shot. If you let yourself get so upset about being in the bunker, or if you rush in to get out in a hurry, you'll have little chance of becoming consistent in your sand play. Take time to plan the shot based on all the observations you have made. And once having planned it, go ahead and follow your plan. Don't second guess yourself. Just like everywhere else on the course you have a good chance of hitting it close from the sand with a confident swing pattern executed in good smooth tempo.

Having evaluated the situation, choose a spot in the sand behind the ball where you want your club to hit on the forward swing. Remember you do not want to hit the ball cleanly but rather take out a cushion of sand on which the ball rides. Therefore you need to look at the spot during your swing, not at the ball. If the ball is sitting up on the sand, you want to make a shallow divot through the sand. But if it is buried partially in the sand, you will have a deeper divot to get the ball out. Plan the angle of your club's attack to give you the shot and divot necessary for the shot.

Set up with your stance slightly open and the clubface slightly open for a basic, shallow-divot shot. Take this position into consideration when aiming and avoid aiming right of the target. Visualize the entire shot. Take time to dig your feet into a solid footing to give you some additional support in the unstable surface of the sand. Swing the club in a slightly outside-in pattern, cutting across the target line. And swing the club back with an early cock of the wrists to get the angle of attack coming down more vertically through the sand. But, and this is a big BUT, don't just swing the club back by cocking the wrists. Go ahead and turn the shoulders. Many golfers are in such a hurry to get out of the sand that they never complete the backswing or the follow-through. Let the weight shift back during the swing but move it back to the left side early in the downswing. And, as in all precision shots, keep the head really still and steady throughout the shot.

On the downswing you should make sure you're pulling the club down and forward with the left hand and arm. Keep the swing going until both hands are above your left shoulder. Remember, as Patty Berg said, ''Swing

HIGH to watch it fly.'' And if it doesn't fly from a bunker, you'll more often than not be still in it or in one on the other side of the green.

You keep hearing me say the same things: steady head, left side control, shift the weight. That's simply because these are the fundamentals of all golf swings. Other fundamentals you'll keep hearing me stress are those of swinging in tempo and without undue tension. When you're in that bunker it may well be a tense situation. Not many golfers would choose to be there. But letting that tension cause you to hold onto the club so tightly that you can't cock the wrists early in the backswing or can't make a total shoulder turn will create even more problems for you. Take the moment necessary to tune in to your body. Relax the shoulders and lighten the grip enough to feel the swing and the shot. Give yourself the advantage of a practice swing on the grass before going into the bunker to review the smooth tempo at which you want to swing. Take that deep breath and then just let the whole program roll off automatically. You'll be surprised that it really will work. And you may find with additional practice you'll be able to say with Ben Hogan, ''The more I practice, the luckier I get.''

DIFFICULT WEATHER CONDITIONS

Unless you play a lot of organized competitive golf, the worst weather conditions under which you play may be wind and cold. Most recreational golfers stop when the rains start. And some won't play if it's too cold or too hot. My advice to you is this: You have to practice what you expect to play in. If you're a golf team member and you know you'll play come what may, then get out into some of those extremes and play a round or two in them. If you know the club championship is coming up and it's likely to be 100 degrees in the shade, then play in it. You simply cannot expect your body, mind and golf swing to immediately adjust to conditions that are totally foreign to what they expect golf conditions to be.

And you cannot expect to be able to adjust unless you are prepared with the proper fundamental techniques and the proper kinds of clothing and equipment.

EXTREME HEAT

Playing in extrerme heat can be a problem if you're inside in air conditioning all week and then come out to play golf on the weekend. Because your muscles will be loose and relaxed in warm weather, the physical aspects of the golf swing are easier in the heat than in the cold. But the heat can not only sap your energy, it can also physically harm you without proper precautions. Wear light colored or white clothing. Wear a hat or visor. Keep a wet towel around your neck or nearby to sponge off your face and neck. Drink lots of liquids, preferably plain old water. Don't wait til you're thirsty, start before then with the water. Stand in the shade when possible. Consider using a riding golf car to save your strength and energy. Be tuned in to your body's signals. If it says it's had enough, consider stopping for the day.

EXTREME COLD

Getting in those last few rounds each fall or the first ones in the spring sometimes puts you out in some pretty nippy weather. Dress for it. Layers of light warm clothing help insulate you without providing so much bulk you can't swing properly. A hat is not only your best friend in hot weather it keeps you from losing a tremendous amount of body heat in cold weather. On really cold days a ski cap works well. Oversized mitts for your hands between shots help keep the feeling and sensitivity you need there for shot-making. And your trusty rain suit can provide an extra layer of insulation when you need just a little more protection.

Your muscles will be tighter in cold weather. This not only makes it difficult to make a smooth, full swing, it also increases danger of injury.

So make sure you warm up by stretching, swinging slowly, and maybe even a little jogging in place before getting up and ripping at it.

You've got to pay close attention to completing your backswing and follow-through when the muscles are tight and cold. The tendency is to get short and jerky. And when the ball misses the sweet spot on a club it will be felt more in cold weather. Changing your expectation level a bit during the cold play helps. The ball will not travel so far and your swing will probably be a little shorter, so allow for that. Use one or two more clubs rather than trying to force your best July distance out of a November swing. Play within yourself and with the weather, not against it.

RAIN

For some people playing golf in the rain would be extreme torture. I admit it's not the most pleasant experience but it can be done efficiently with planning. First of all, it goes without saying that if there is any lightning accompanying the rain, don't even stop to consider playing. Get out of those dangerous conditions immediately. Do not let yourself be talked into ignoring them. Get into shelter right away. If there is no lightning and you are playing in the rain, be prepared. Wear a rain suit and waterproof shoes if at all possible. If the rain is warm and you do not mind getting wet, then the rain suit may not appeal to you. But keep your equipment dry if not yourself. Golf gloves and club grips both can get very slippery if you do not keep them dry. If you know that you will be competing in potentially rainy conditions, you should purchase an all weather golf glove that remains fairly tacky when wet. Keeping an umbrella over your clubs will prevent water from running down into the bag and getting them even wetter. And keeping a towel hung from the inside of the umbrella will keep it dry for you to dry your hands and club grips.

Having taken care of your physical needs and your equipment, you'll have to address yourself to playing the game now. Keep a positive outlook.

Everyone out there is playing under the same conditions, so no one has any advantage over you. Fundamental skills will serve you well in ideal conditions and less than ideal. Get away from thinking about how bad it is. Think how you can make the best of it.

Knowing a couple of facts about wet weather play gives you a head start on handling it. Anytime you are playing a shot in wet conditions, even heavy dew, you will have the chance of having water on the clubface at impact. This produces less spin on the ball so it's likely to go lower and longer than it would under dry conditions. The second problem you'll face in playing in the rain is keeping your footing stable. Make sure you set up to the ball with a balanced, good stance and if it is really wet, take only a three-quarter swing. At any rate, you must make sure that your swing is slow, smooth and easy so that you won't lose your balance. And finally you want to make sure that you don't hit the ball fat but that you contact the ball cleanly, sweeping it off the grass.

Since the ball is already flying lower and longer because of reduced spin you really don't want to move it back any further in your stance the way you do for some other recovery shots. Instead, simply swing with an easy motion, keeping the body extremely steady, and try to sweep the ball off the turf. Just reading that should make you see why it's important to practice this type of shot. Control of anxiety and the urge to see the results help you make this swing a sound one. Use more club and swing easier and accept more playable misses. Playing in the rain makes you appreciate how relatively simple a swing on a sunny day can be!

One other fundamental to keep in mind for playing in the rain is that of knowing your legal options under the "casual water" rule. Remember that if any water is visible either before or after you take your stance, you can get relief from that lie. And you can move the ball as far as necessary, to the nearest point, no closer to the hole, to get that relief. Another bonus to getting this relief is that you are allowed to clean your ball when you pick it up to drop it out of the casual water. Many times knowing and using this rule will give you a much better lie from which to play. It's just one example of how the rules can help you to play better if you know them well and when to use them.

WIND

Unfortunately, there are no rules to help you play in the wind, at least not in the USGA Rules Book. But there are some fundamental guidelines to help you.

The old adage of "Swing easy when it's breezy" is one of the very best pieces of advice you can get for playing in the wind. Playing in the wind, like playing under any other sort of different conditions, can make you want to push, to force things, to swing fast and hard, to shorten the backswing. All of these things will ruin your shotmaking ability in the wind. Your first general fundamental that must be adhered to it is to set up in your best balanced position and then make your best, full swing pattern without rushing it. Then simply adjust your expectation level for the conditions. Just like rain, the wind can take its toll on everyone's score. Keeping an even mental keel and playing one shot at the time helps you win each battle and finally even the war.

If the wind is so strong as to make you feel like you're losing your balance during your swing, you may need to widen your stance to increase your base of support. But remember once you do that you make it harder to turn and therefore you won't get the full value of your swing so you'll lose distance. Taking one or two additional clubs will make it easy to adjust to this situation.

Three different kinds of wind cause three different types of problems. Headwinds add to the lift of the ball, causing it to go higher and shorter. From your swing standpoint, it makes it harder to transfer your weight and complete your swing without paying close attention to doing that.

CHAPTER SIX

Make yourself hold your body steady during the backswing. The tendency will be to sway away from the ball with the wind direction. And cue in on your footwork to get the weight and swing moving back toward the target side with a strong move. If you have the skills to play different types of ball flights, you should try to draw the ball from right to left into a headwind. You will remember when we were talking about the players who grew up on the windswept links courses and played this type of shot to keep the ball below the wind.

Tailwinds seem like they would be a real aid to your game. But as you know, long is not always better. Swinging in a following wind makes it easy for you to rush that forward part of the swing if you aren't careful to stay in good tempo throughout the whole swing pattern. And with a following wind the ball is going to be harder to stop once it hits the ground. You have to take that into consideration when you're playing with the wind behind you. You'll need to chose a club or two less for the following wind shots, but don't forget to go ahead and accelerate the swing. You want this ball to get into the wind, you don't want to take any chances in holding back and babying the shot. Nor do you want to try to over-control the swing and try to steer the ball downwind. Go ahead and commit yourself to a club and a swing then try to complete it with good accelerating tempo. Nothing too different about that thought, is it? Just keep it foremost in your mind when playing with a tailwind.

Crosswinds sometimes give you the most problems of all. Again you have to make a decision on how to play your shot before attempting it. If you can control the flight of your ball easily, then you may choose to hook or slice the shot into the wind to keep it on line against the wind. Most weekend golfers will be more successful if they would just aim left or right of the target, opposite the way the wind is blowing, and let the wind blow the ball back toward the target.

Besides the basic adjustments you make for any wind shot, you need to trust your decision-making abilities in playing in a crosswind. Choose a target that you think is far enough left or right to allow for the wind and then go ahead and swing with conviction.

Remember one more thing about playing in the wind. It can be very physically and mentally tiring. Keep your energy and strength up by resting at tees or in a cart between shots. Keep your thought processes sharp. Evaluate all conditions. But always keep a realistic, positive outlook. That will serve you as well as any other fundamental in playing shots in the wind. And that attitude is important when playing shots that demand you get the ball under, over, around or away from some kind of obstacle(s).

SHOTS THAT GO UNDER, OVER, AROUND, OR AWAY FROM . . . WHATEVER

I've said that you need a realistic, positive attitude to get out of some of these kinds of situations. The other thing you need is enough imagination to see possibilities for recovery and enough realism to evaluate those possibilities. And finally you need to have the skills with which to execute the shots.

TO GO UNDER

When you find yourself in a situation demanding that you hit the ball lower than you normally would, there are a couple of basic things to do. The most obvious one is to simply choose a lower numbered, less lofted club, choke down on the grip and hit a sort of chip shot with a low followthrough. If that still isn't low enough, then move the ball back in your stance, keep the hands ahead and swing in a very shallow arc. That should keep any shot low. Remember, even a strong rolling shot that gets you out of whatever you're in is a great shot, for that circumstance. Recovery shots don't have to be pretty to be loved!

119

CHAPTER SIX

TO GO OVER

Going over an obstacle may mean you have to choose a more lofted club and therefore sacrifice some distance to get the necessary height. That takes us right back to good course management: Play the lie first, the obstacles second and the distance as your third priority. Don't lose sight of those relative priorities.

If choosing a more lofted club still is not enough height, then you can add more trajectory by moving the ball forward in your stance and swinging with a steep angle of attack. Putting the ball forward allows it to go off the top of the clubface when the clubface itself is laid back. That increases the loft of the club. As with your other shots, keep the arms swinging to a high finish to insure maximum trajectory of the ball's flight.

TO GO AROUND

To maneuver the ball around an obstacle you need to know how to hook and slice a ball. Knowing what contributes to those ball flights and then spending your time on the practice tee working on them gives you the best chance for success during play. But keep one thing in mind. Before you start planning a shot requiring a lot of spin be placed on the ball by the clubface, check out your lie. If you're in tall grass or any area where the grass is likely to get between your clubface and the ball, don't expect much hook or slice to result. The material between the ball and club will prevent the spin from affecting the ball flight.

Knowing that you need to get the toe of the club to the ball before the heel of the club in order to hook it tells you how to use your hands in a situation where you try to hook. The path along which you swing can be easily chosen also. Here's a good rule of thumb: Set up your stance so that your foot line is parallel to the opening you want to hit toward. Swing along that line. Take the club in your normal grip but with the clubface facing the obstacle, not square to the target line. This in effect sets you up with a closed clubface so you don't have to do a lot of manipulation during the swing.

If you wanted to slice around an obstacle, then set up with your foot line running to the left of the obstacle and the clubface facing the obstacle. Swing along your foot line. You have to practice this over and over to feel comfortable doing it. And unless you can feel comfortable and can have the confidence of knowing it will work, you will never have the confidence to use it during play.

TO GO AWAY FROM

When you have to get your ball out away from some type of obstacle, you may really have to be inventive. Getting out from under low hanging branches may require an extremely wide stance and a low swing that goes around from ankle to ankle, literally.

Getting away from an obstacle on the left side of the ball may require playing the shot backwards from the right side of your body or hitting the ball with the back of your clubhead left-handed.

Getting away from a long obstacle, such as the side of a building may mean you have to close the clubface before you swing and trust the ball to go really left and of course low as well.

Getting away from tree roots may mean almost putting the ball off the areas so as not to injure your hands or break your club.

Getting away from the water's edge will mean you have to take a highly lofted club and swing in a very steep pattern up and down to get it out of the muddy water area.

Getting away from any trouble always follows one fundamental rule. First of all, make sure you will end up in better shape than you're in now. If you can't guarantee that then simply take your one-stroke penalty for an unplayable lie and put your mind on planning the best place, under your legal options, to drop the ball and put it back in play. Remember to decide what you're going to do before picking up the ball. Once you've decided to take the penalty stroke and drop and have then picked up the ball, you have to proceed with that plan. You can't put it back and decide to go ahead and play it.

Using the unplayable lie rule gives you the option of dropping the ball two club-lengths in any direction, so long as it isn't closer to the hole, from the spot where the ball has come to rest. It doesn't necessarily mean that that will put you out of trouble, you see. So evaluate that option as compared to the others. You also have the option of dropping the ball anywhere along an imaginary line extending from the flagstick through where the ball is sitting, all the way to the boundary of the golf course. Any spot along that line that is *behind* where the ball sits, that is. And, of course, you can always go right back to the last spot you hit the ball. If you've just failed on a recovery shot and that has put you further "in jail," you may want to take the ball back to that spot and try the recovery shot over. Of course, all of the options carry the one-stroke penalty for an unplayable lie just like the two-club-length option.

SUMMARY

No golfer can escape having to play shots from troublesome situations on a course. The better you can prepare yourself with a variety of fundamental modifications, a knowledge of conditions, a knowledge of rules of golf, and with self-control and intelligent analyses, the better equipped you will be to play these shots.

Keeping a cool head. Using basic fundamentals. Maintaining good smooth tempo. Trusting your decision and your swing. These are the necessary ingredients for good recovery golf. You can learn some of them intellectually. You must practice all of them regularly. Like every other aspect of your game, there is no substitute for good instruction, good practice and good old experience either on the practice tee or in the game.

As they say, "You can pay me now or you can pay me later." Practicing recovery skills allow you to pay your dues when it doesn't hurt your score. Not practicing them costs you strokes. You choose when you'll learn these skills.

CHAPTER SEVEN
Mental Skills in Play

———————

You know now that the things I believe you need to play this game well are really quite simple. You need to understand the skills you're trying to develop and you need to practice those skills. And you need to use your head. I've said before that Jack Nicklaus does that so well. You can improve yourself in this area also.

INTELLECTUAL SKILLS

Throughout this whole book I have been cautioning you to plan, to think through shots and results. That's part of what using your brain is all about. The thinking golfer, that's what you want to be. I don't mean it has to be all work out there. Far from it. I agree with Walter Hagen when he said we should all stop and smell the flowers along the way. But when you get ready to play a shot, commit yourself to that project right then and there with all your attention.

Everyone plays the game according to his or her own personality. Trevino plays very differently from Nicklaus. But both of them, and you, need to focus your attention on the task at hand when it comes time to hit a shot. The remainder of a golf round, about two thirds to three quarters of the actual time on the course, can be spent in whatever way you choose to spend it, talking business, joking with friends, or in quiet enjoyment and contemplation.

No matter what your physical skills in the game you can use good intellectual prowess from the very beginning of your play. Learn to use a pre-shot routine in the same way that a basketball player uses a certain number of bounces before every foul shot. Use your routine to signal the mind and body to get ready to play a golf shot. At the beginning of the routine all attention is now on planning and executing your shot.

You won't see a professional player who doesn't use one. It may be unique such as Hubie Green's up-and-downs. It may be almost casual like Joanne Carner's step up and fire. But it has two qualities that are always present. Yours must have the same qualities: You must aim the ball and you must prepare your body for movement.

Most routines start when you select the club from your bag. How you go about it from there is very personal. The important thing is not so much what you do as it is that you do the same thing and at the same tempo every time. That includes those shots from trouble as well as the ones from the fairway. You have to use the same routine when you step up to the ball after firing two shots out of bounds that you use on the tee after making a birdie on the last hole. And you have to have a routine for putting, approach shots, irons and woods. All shots need that signal from the mind to the body.

A very real part of that signal is using another intellectual facet, visualization. Not only is it important to visualize your approach shots and your putts, it is equally important to visualize your drives and full shots with other clubs, too. That's all part of what gets the body ready to move, to make that visualized shot a reality.

Once again, your abilities to vividly imagine the shot you want to make, your swing and the results, need to be practiced. They need to be used in informal play as well as competition. You need to make visualization as detailed as possible.

Some players tell me they don't use a routine and go through all of that stuff because it slows up play. I always ask them how much they think three bad shots in a row slow up play. A routine won't guarantee that you'll never have a bad shot, but it sure will make it easier to have a good one. And it shouldn't necessarily take a long time. Studies of touring professionals show that their entire routine from taking the club out of the bag to hitting the ball, takes somewhere between eight and 13 seconds, surely not enough time to hold up play.

Even though the routine is the signal for the body to actually start the shot, there are other intellectual and mental processes necessary before that moment. A lot of them are simple to define and you find yourself agreeing with me. But in actual play I see a lot of golfers NOT doing them. Making a decision, you'll no doubt agree, is a part of using your head in golf. But making the decision and then sticking by it with no second guessing, that's what makes you a GOOD golfer.

There's no guarantee with most golf shots. Luck will always play a part, a good bounce, a lucky miss, a bad break. They're part of the game, part of what makes it exciting. But unless you, the player, have a plan based on the best information you have and unless you commit yourself to that plan without trying to steer the ball and control the results, you'll have little chance of repeating success. So do you see how important it is to have good fundamental skills so you can trust them?

Making a successful golf swing, in fact a series of them, demands that you learn to "push a button," that is use some sort of verbal and physical cue for the swing and then just let it go. That can be downright scary. But it is a skill you must develop.

To prove it to yourself how important it is to trust your decisions and your past learning of skills try this little experiment. Take a piece of paper and sign your name, just like you were signing a check or letter. Then, below that, try to perfectly copy your signature. Don't cheat and just whip off another signature. Rather, go ahead and pay close attention to your original signature and copy it as precisely as you can. Now on a third line simply sign your name again. As you look at the three lines I'll bet you find there may not be as much difference between lines 1 and 3 as there is between lines 1 and 2. "Trying to be perfect," as in copying, usually produces more variations, And it probably took you far longer to work your way through copying the signature than it did to simply sign your name. If you had a videotape of yourself doing it you would have also seen a lot of pressure and tension in your hand.

This little experiment shows you what happens when you try to consciously *control* any physical skill with your mind. It's the same with your golf swing. When you try to think your way through the entire swing, when you try to analyze every move, you are likely to have no more success than when you tried to copy your name. You have to practice letting it happen, making that choice and then trusting it to work.

Golfers are some of the worst people for learning to give up this control of every tiny detail of the swing. Once you learn to swim you don't expect to have to think your way through every arm and leg action to keep from drowning. Once you've learned to ride a bike, even if you haven't ridden a bike in years, you'll go ahead and get on and ride a few blocks without crashing. But you won't trust that golf swing to work. It's the same thing, a skill you've learned and a skill you must trust. Your energy needs to be directed toward strategy and tactics of playing the game. Part of what makes it hard to trust your golf swing is your outlook on the game. Controlling that outlook is one of the most important mental exercises you can do for yourself.

Look at the best hitter in professional baseball. He's batting around .350 or .380 if he's lucky. That means he's 35% to 38% successful. And he's the best of all the professionals. But golfers, amateurs at that, expect to bat a clean 1.000 . . . perfect, no bad shots, and no misses. It's certainly not a very realistic viewpoint of the game. Convince yourself that you, too, will have a batting average for that round and that day. And, while it will never be 1.000, it can be high enough for you to accomplish your goals and objectives for that round. Even Al Geiberger, after shooting his record-setting 59 at the Colonial in Memphis, said he knew of several shots he could have ''saved'' had he hit them better!''

One of the things that will help you control that outlook is to have a game plan. Ben Hogan reportedly would go through a course he was going to play and plan the holes he thought he could birdie, the ones he could risk trying to birdie, and the ones he'd play for par. While your level of play may be different from Hogan's you can set yourself a game plan. At your own home course spend a little time before your next round planning your overall game. Look at where you can gamble without risking everything. Plan the placement of shots. Be realistic about your own skills. Map out the highest percentage shots.

Now, one word of caution here. I've seen golfers who set up their game plan and then start to panic if their play begins to vary from it. Remember, it is only a plan and if one shot or one hole varies from it, it does not mean the whole game is falling apart. Regroup, go back to playing well within yourself. Do not compound one error with another. And soon you'll see the game plan come back into focus.

That whole idea of playing within yourself and only one shot at the time is another skill you really have to work on. It's a game of the present! If your energies and attention are completely focused on what you are doing, you have little time for dwelling on what went wrong in the past or for planning too far down the road of the future.

You have to know where you want to hit the next shot because that tells you where to aim this one. Think about it, now. Knowing where you want to place the next shot tells you where it must be hit from and that tells you the point of aim for this one. It's called setting up the hole. And it's part of smart mental planning. You can't plan to get a par on this hole on the tee. Oh yes, it may well be part of your overall game plan to get a par on this hole because it's within your ability to do so. But on the tee all you have time and energy for is aiming the tee shot to a spot from which you want to hit your next shot, and cueing yourself for your very best swing.

That's easy enough to do if your game plan is going along successfully. But it's harder to do when you've just had a three-putt for a double bogey on the last hole. It's even harder to do when you've just chipped in for a birdie on the last hole. That's why you need to practice it. Play in lots of competitions if you want to become a better player. Get that experience of using mental and physical skills in the competitive arena. It's the only way to improve your competitive skills.

Another reason to always keep your mind on the present is to keep you from being overly score conscious. The bottom line for most players in golf is learning to play better so that they can improve their scores. You're probably no different. One of the things that sometimes keeps you from doing that is something called your "comfort zone." That's the area in which you are most at home, the range of scores that you subconsciously feel is right for you. And that comfort zone can block you from breaking 100, breaking 90, breaking 80 or whatever your goal currently is.

Think about it. Do you ever play a really good front nine and a bad back nine? Or a bad front and good back? How about those high scores on 8 and 9 and/or on 16, 17 and 18? Or, if you aren't playing too well that day, they may be really GOOD scores on those holes. It may be nothing more than your mind putting you right back in to that area of acceptable scores.

But as a thinking, intelligent golfer you can break the cycle. You have to keep playing the game one shot at the time, minimizing your awareness of the overall picture. As many professionals have learned, if you take care of the individual shots, the numbers will take care of themselves. Recognize the potential for a big number when you get into trouble. Make yourself play the shot with the highest recovery percentage. Take a moment to compose yourself before rushing up and playing the next shot after a bad one. Stay in the present.

Golf really is a game of reducing disasters and not a game of playing perfection. That's not a negative outlook. Just think if you never had a triple bogey during a round you'd never score over 108. If you never had a double bogey, you'd never score over 90 and if you never had more than nine bogeys you'd never post more than an 81. Knowing that puts the game in perspective. But you can't think about it during play. It takes your attention away from the present. The game is played in the present, two shots at the time.

Another reason for keeping your attention focused clearly on what you're doing in the present is that it prevents you from spending a lot of energy worrying about opponents. Directing your attention to your game and not being influenced by either the good or bad play of others is another skill you need to master. Go right back to your basic psychology: You can't control what the other player does (or how he or she acts) but you can control how you react to him or her. Golf is a game played primarily between you and the golf course. Even in match play. Learn to play YOUR game. That is the only way you can make sure of your best effort.

And going along with that is the necessity of keeping your attention focused on the shot at hand in order to prevent yourself from over-reacting to your own emotions. Notice I said ''over-reacting.'' It's natural for you to have some reaction during play. But allowing the emotions of fear or anxiety, anger, over-excitement, dejection or any other strong feeling to adversely affect your play will spell disaster for even the best round. Learning to reocognize and cope with emotion during play is an entire area of mental golf in itself. For many players, maybe even you, it is the one area in which they are weakest. But luckily, just like every other skill of playing this game, learning to control emotions and have them work positively for yourself improves with instruction, discipline and practice.

EMOTIONAL SKILLS

Golf can be a frustrating game. Everyone who plays it knows that. Not everyone who plays it accepts that. Almost everyone who plays it wants to improve. If you do, then you must make sure that you practice emotional control as much as you practice chipping.

Tom Watson says he believes everyone who plays the game gets mad at some time. That in itself is understandable. How you choose to react to this anger and frustration will be a mark of yourself as a thinking golfer. Ignoring emotions in golf does not teach you how to cope with them. Trying to ignore something that is really there is a futile exercise, only adding to your frustration level. Prove it to yourself this way. For 30 seconds try to forget the number ''7.'' Don't think ''7.'' Pretend that ''7'' no longer exists and that you'll never have to use ''7'' again even though every week has 7 days, etc. You get the idea. The more you try to forget something that's still present, the more impossible it becomes.

Ignoring anger, then, will not work. What will work is to tell yourself literally, ''Stop!'' That specific word works very well because we're so conditioned to it and what it means. ''Stop'' only means stop. Quit what you're doing. And what you're doing is wasting energy over something that is in the past. Golf has no past, only the present. You know, it's the old ''all the king's horses and all the king's men can't put Humpty Dumpty back together again,'' theory. You can't help that triple bogey or even that dumb shot that you just made. So ''stop'' thinking about it. Clear your mind of those angry thoughts that are cluttering up the space you need to be using to plan *this* shot or to play this hole.

It's not easy to gather yourself and remove angry feelings. Part of the reason is that sometimes the anger exists because we feel inadequate and stupid for making such a ''dumb'' mistake. It doesn't necessarily help at the moment to know that everyone who plays the game has at one time or another had the same problems. But that is part of your learning to cope with these kinds of emotions. Make yourself more aware of when you start getting upset and angry during play. Use the ''stop''mechanism. And keep practicing it. Bobby Jones was known early in his career for losing emotional control. But like every successful golfer he had to learn to control his emotions. You can do it too. Like everything else, practicing the fundamental skills of control will make it work for you.

Another emotion that can interfere with clear thinking is old-fashioned fear. That nervousness of playing in a big event, or of playing with new people, or of just playing in front of people, or of playing really well (or really poorly) . . . any of those things can give you a real problem in golf. Muscles get tight. The grip clenches. The palms sweat. The heart races. And the mind goes blank. The results? It could be a swing the speed of light which has no chance for success. Or a swing so short that you lose much of your distance. Or a shot that no one in his right mind would try. Have you forgotten how to play the game? No, you're just nervous.

Nervousness or anxiety are sometimes present even when you don't realize it. Your best cure for it is to do two things: prepare as well as you can by having your physical skills well honed; and learn some basic coping skills for dealing with nervousness. For most competitors a little nervousness helps you get ''up'' for a match or a tournament. Tune in to your body to feel the difference between the high level of awareness when you're ''ready'' and the crippling nervousness that is too much. Only you can control it, but you will never be able to do that unless you can first recognize it.

The best way of coping with anxiety, whether it is over a single shot or over an entire tournament, is to learn to take very deep, slow breaths feeling your muscles relax while you are doing so. The body will automatically relax when you breathe deeply and slowly. Sometimes forcing yourself to tense up muscle groups, like hunching up your shoulders and then relaxing them, will help remove muscular tension. But the greatest way of coping is still to have prepared yourself through practice of fundamentals so that you have enough confidence in your skills to know you are capable of playing well, whatever "well" is for you.

Knowing what that "playing well" is, or should I say, accepting what it is, takes some hard analysis. I guess everyone who plays the game echos the feeling of the fellow who said, "I wish I could play my normal game just once!" But you fool no one when you overestimate your abilities, least of all yourself. There's no shame in playing the game to the best of your abilities, whatever they are at this time. But because the game LOOKS a lot easier than it is, you sometimes expect that you should be doing a lot better.

If golf were really that easy, don't you think the pros would be shooting in the 50s and even 40s by now? They surely can hit the ball long enough. Their skills are honed daily. But they, like you, still have to play the game as one individual against the course and against themselves.

Learning to accept yourself and your skill is as important as learning to hit a bunker shot. Keeping the perspective that it is indeed a game you're playing out there. It is not a life and death struggle. Play it the absolute best you can. Think your way through it. Use the skills you've learned. And analyze your strengths and weaknesses afterward to be able to play better in the future.

Practice your mental skills as much as your physical ones. Use your brain as an asset to complement your techniques of play. Spend time learning about the game. Spend time learning about yourself. And spend time working to improve all aspects of playing the game. You'll see good, positive results begin to happen. And that will produce lower scores!

THE LEGENDARY PATTY BERG, *after finishing last in her first tournament (the Minneapolis City Championship), came back the following year to win the event. She did this by analyzing her strengths and weaknesses, then working to make her weaknesses strengths.*

CHAPTER EIGHT

Conditioning Yourself to Play

Golf is not often thought of as being one of the more active sports. In fact it sometimes is laughed at by the "jocks." But anyone who plays the game well knows that golf requires more from the body than it appears to.

You can often help yourself lower your scores by following certain conditioning guidelines. And by that I mean all phases of conditioning, including strength building, endurance, and flexibility.

If you are a recreational golfer who works full time you will have limited time for either golf *or* conditioning for golf. But some of the exercises I'm going to suggest can be done without much equipment and without taking up a lot of your time.

Just like learning the skills of the game, conditioning for the games takes commitment, discipline, and practice. If you aren't willing to give those qualities then you cannot expect much in the way of results.

Before getting into specific exercises for golfers let's identify exactly what you need to work on. Strength is important in golf. We know that. Where the strength is located is also important. One area where it is vital that you have enough strength is in the hands and forearms. It has been said that unless you are strong enough in your hands to hold the club lightly without being afraid you'll lose it then you'll always be gripping too tightly. Juniors and women often have to work on grip strength and arm strength.

Strength is also necessary in the legs and lower body. You can't possibly use the legs and feet strongly and actively unless you are strong in these areas. And, if you walk 18 holes of golf, you cannot expect to stay lively on your feet at the end of the round without strong legs.

Part of that staying lively is also related to endurance. I see a lot of golfers lose their games because they simply give out before the round is over. Timing becomes affected. Power is lost. And consistency is almost impossible. Getting tired can happen in muscle groups or to the body as a whole. Cardiovascular endurance is also a factor when the round includes walking, particularly over hilly terrain, and carrying a golf bag. Endurance is also affected by strong winds during play.

And the final area of flexibility is one in which nearly all men need improvement. Because the golf swing is a turning, stretching motion of the body, flexibility is a must. Normally men have less flexibility than women, but more strength. So just as women need to work on building strength, men need to work on flexibility. Sam Snead, in his 70's can still kick high enough to touch the top of a door frame with his toe. That's real flexibility.

The good thing about using a simple program of conditioning for golf is that often you can combine conditioning with golf drills. That is really good if you're on a tight schedule.

One thing that you must always keep in mind before starting to condition for golf or anything else is that you should not just jump into an exercise program. It is always best to check out any program with your doctor before starting it. And it is best to always try to follow a training schedule that gives you a day of exercise and a day of rest. Good common sense will tell you that improving fitness for golf doesn't come any faster than improving your swing. It takes time and practice.

STRENGTH BUILDING
Building strength for golf has really two specific functions. The most

SAM SNEAD *has worked continuously to maintain his flexibility. That has contributed to his longevity as a player.*

obvious one is to be able to play better, hit the ball further, and have better control of your golf swing. But there's an equally important second reason: To prevent injury.

You may not have thought much about injury in golf and yet it happens. The back, shoulders and hands are the most susceptible muscle groups. Increasing strength in these areas, as well as in the body as a whole will help you avoid injury.

If you belong to a health club or work out with weight training machinery regularly, there are some specific exercises that contribute to overall body strength, particularly in the areas most used for golf.

The PGA of America has researched various programs using the Nautilus type of progressive resistance machinery. The advantage of this type of training machinery is that it works as much on flexibility as it does on strength. For a golfer this is a must in any program.

The following program is suggested as an inclusive one.[1] If you aren't already involved in Nautilus training, you have to start with less resistance and work up to this optimum training level. This program should be done every other day if possible:

Raise on toes-Multi machine . . . . 100 lbs.

Leg extension . . . . 50 lbs.

Leg curl . . . . 40 lbs.

Hip and back . . . . 65 lbs.

Hip flexion . . . . 40 lbs.

Back extension . . . . 120 lbs.

Abduction . . . . 60 lbs.

Adduction . . . . 60 lbs.

Rotary torso . . . . 75 lbs.

Double shoulder machine-lateral raise . . . . 50 lbs.

[1]*PGA Magazine*, Research of Dr. Stan Plagenhoef and Dr. Gary Wiren, Vol. 64, No. 2, February, 1983.

Behind neck-torso arm. . . . . .60 lbs.
Pullover . . . . .90 lbs.
Biceps. . . . . .40 lbs.
Triceps . . . . .40 lbs.
Hand flexion-Multi machine extension .60 lbs.
Hand supination/pronation abduction/
adduction (lever bar 5'10'') . . . . .40 lbs.

GREAT GOLF *starts with a flexible, conditioned body.*

CHAPTER EIGHT

The most important exercises are related to the abductors, adductors, medial rotators, and lateral rotators of the thigh and upper arm. The rotators of the trunk and the stabilizers or the forward lean of the trunk — the back extensors. *The most important machines to use then are:*

1. Rotary torso
2. Back extension
3. Hip and back (for lateral rotators as well as extensors)
4. Abductor (also for medial rotators)
5. Adductor (also for lateral rotators)
6. Lateral raise on Double Shoulder machine (abductors and rotators)
7. Behind neck on Behind Neck-Torso Arm machine (adductors & rotators)
8. Pullover (for medial rotators, adductors, and to aid in maintaining muscular balance in the trunk due to the inclusion of the back extension and hip and back exercises)
9. All hand and forearm exercises

Maybe you don't have either the time or inclination to get into conditioning with such a total program as outlined above. But there are other things you can do to maintain and improve your strength in important muscle groups.

For example, to work on those all important leg muscles you can simply walk or even jog whenever possible. That means even when you're on the course. If you and your partner are sharing a golf car, then let him drive while you walk. Or share driving responsibilities so you both can walk at least nine holes. Jack Nicklaus does it even today with every round he plays. I don't think I've ever seen him ride a cart 18 holes.

And walk other places, too. Take that flight of stairs instead of pushing the elevator button. Ride a bike around the block a few times after dinner instead of immediately sitting down for TV. Train the legs by using them and by overloading them. That means using them longer and/or faster than they're used to being used. It's pretty simple but not necessarily fun to do. So make it fun. Go out for a walk with your spouse and enjoy the company and the neighborhood. Play other sports that use your legs. A fast game of handball or tennis will help keep the legs in shape, too.

Exercising and conditioning the legs are somewhat easier than working on the other important muscles for golf. Training the back and trunk muscles sometimes requires more specific activities. But they, too, can be made part of your daily routine, if playing better golf is important to you. Building strength in the muscles around the wasit, the stomach, and lower back can not only help prevent back injury, it can also add to your ability to make a full turn in the golf swing. If just the muscles in your lower back are working during your turn because the stomach and side muscles have given out, you can't turn too well.

So one of your areas for work may be in building better stomach muscles to help support the spine and your turn. Old fashioned sit-ups are not the best way to do this. Instead, try doing body curls. Lie flat on your back with your knees bent and your feet flat on the floor. Push the lower back down to the floor while you lift your shoulders and chest barely off the floor. Raising the shoulders only two to five inches can strengthen the stomach muscles. Hold the position for a count of four and then take another count of four to lower the shoulders. Slow, sustained raising and lowering will provide more work for the muscles. Jerking up and falling down are extremely inefficient ways to do this exercise.

Other exercises to add both strength and flexibility to these trunk muscles include lying flat on your back then pushing the lower back into the floor. Hold that position for five seconds and relax. Standing with the feet shoulder width apart, you can tilt your body as far over to one side as possible, from the waist. Slowly pull the body back to the upright position. Let your hand and arm fall over your head to add extra resistance for the pull back to position. Do this about 10 or 20 times on both sides.

CHAPTER EIGHT

And a particularly good exercise for not only strengthening the back slightly but also for just making it feel better is a reverse upward curl. Stand with feet shoulder width apart. Allow entire upper body to bend as far forward as possible from the waist. Slowly straighten up feeling every vertebrae come up separately from bottom to top of spine. Then stretch high with your arms above your head. Do this a number of times every day just to help relax your back and yourself, too.

Working on the shoulder girdle can often be combined with work on the arms and hands. Because of the difference in body structure, women are less strong in the upper body. Therefore, women should spend some time developing additional strength in these areas to make the game easier. Using light resistance such as arm weights or small bar bells can overload the arm and shoulder muscles to the point where you can get some benefits. Even holding a golf club at full length can become heavy sometimes.

Swinging a weighted golf club is one of the best training techniques you can use to strengthen this area of the body. You can make your own trainer club by buying lead tape and adding it to an old golf club. Make sure that you don't make the club so heavy that you'll sprain your wrists or thumbs while swinging it. To get maximum benefits from this type of device you should swing for a number of repetitions, say 20, then rest a couple of minutes and swing again. Because small muscles will tire before you notice fatigue in large ones, don't overdo so that you lose good technique. Swinging this type of club also assists you in developing a bigger and better turn because the weight of the club forces you to swing it.

Other types of informal training for these muscles groups includes holding a club at arm's length and rotating it a full 180 degrees. Use both the left and right hands for this drill. Do several repetitions with each hand. You can also hold the club out in front of you and lift it to a vertical position using only your wrist. Ten or 20 repetitions of this drill is necessary for you to overload muscles and thereby get some training effects.

Swinging a club with only the left arm and actually hitting golf balls with just the left hand on the club is another excellent conditioning drill with good application to your game. Use a short or middle iron and start with just swinging the club. Once you feel yourself able to control the club, start hitting shots with the one-armed swing.

Squeezing a tennis ball or some other rubber ball while on the phone or driving to work can help you build grip strength. This is particularly good for ladies. But almost everyone who plays the game can benefit from having strong hands.

ENDURANCE

Endurance is that quality which allows your muscles to keep working. Endurance is one of the things that can help keep you from getting those big numbers near the end of the round when your swing seems to lose something. And endurance in small muscle groups is what keeps your swing from falling apart.

It is obviously related to strength but endurance is certainly more than strength. You will need some special training to help yourself maximize your endurance potential.

Professional golfers hit balls for hours, play 18 holes of golf and maybe even hit more balls almost every day. That in itself builds endurance. But most of you don't have that kind of intensive golf schedule. You need something else to help you stay totally fit.

If you follow the comprehensive Nautilus workout described earlier in this chapter you will find your endurance also getting better. But if you are going to be doing a less intensive program the following activities will contribute to your endurance training.

Walking, running, jogging or any other activity that increases your heart rate will help you build better cardio-vascular endurance. But again a word of caution. Don't start an intensive cardio-vascular workout program without clearing it with your doctor. And remember that walking 2½ miles five times a week gives you the same workout that running 2 miles three times a week does. Generally, unless you're already in pretty good shape, you want to keep your pulse rate between 120 and 140 beats per minute. Raising it higher than that should be avoided.

This cardio-vascular endurance is what will allow you to still feel rested at the end of the round. If golf is the only activity you have during the week, you cannot expect that to provide the training necessary to keep you fit. Remember you have to overload the body, that is work it harder than normal, for training to take place. And you have to keep working at it to maintain that level of training.

A rule of thumb for you is that it will take about a month of training, three times a week for every year you've been out of shape, to get yourself back into shape. That's not meant to discourage you. But rather it's meant to spur you into starting today. If lack of basic endurance is the only thing standing in the way of your shooting lower numbers, that's one of the simplest things to "fix." Besides that, it will just be all-around good for you.

The other kind of endurance that you need for golf is muscle endurance. As I mentioned earlier, if the stomach muscles give out then your back can be injured. If small muscles in the hands and forearms tire, then tendons can be pulled. Following a program of strength building for each muscle group will also contribute to your building endurance in them. The basic rule of conditioning is to do heavy work for fewer repetitions to build strength and to do lighter work for a greater number of repetitions, or sets of repetitions for more endurance training.

Some of the strength building work like swinging the weighted club will most definitely add to your muscle endurance as well. Try to select those exercises that will give you gain in both areas.

FLEXIBILITY

Without good flexibility it is very hard to play golf well. Your basic body type will help determine the amount of flexibility you have. But almost everyone who's not already a dancer or a gymnast can increase their range of movement.

The most important thing you should keep in mind about flexibility training is how to go about it without injuring yourself or putting yourself in a lot of pain. The old saying of "no pain — no gain" is not really all that true. Even when you work to increase flexibility, you should do it with the same conservative approach that you use in strength and endurance training.

Incorrect technique for increasing range of motion, such as bouncing or bobbing, can cause you to tear muscles and may actually cause the muscles to tighten instead of stretch. To increase flexibility you need to do a full range of stretching exercises. Because maintaining flexibility is so important to everyone as we age, it is a good habit to get into. Two or three times a week you should spend 15 to 20 minutes in stretching. And before you do any other kind of exercise, including golf, you should stretch out and warm up fully to prevent injury and muscle damage.

The correct technique for working on your flexibility is to stretch fully as far as you can go without pain and then hold that position for 15 or 20 seconds. Each exercise should be repeated a minimum of 10 times. And each time you should strive to stretch further than the time before.

Specific body areas that need increased flexibility for golf include the shoulders, neck, back, hips and hamstrings. Although there are lots of different stretching exercises you can do for each one these areas I'll give you a few examples to get you started.

Injury to shoulder joints is less likely to occur when the surrounding muscles are strong and the joint itself flexible. Holding a golf club high over your head with one hand at either end of the shaft, try to bring the club down behind your neck. I repeat, don't force it so far as to cause injury. Another variation on that is to take the club behind you at chest height. Loop the thumbs over the shaft with your palms facing away from your body. Not only can you feel the stretch from that initial position, you can also hold the club there and turn the entire torso left and right, stretching still other important golf muscles.

Clasping your fingers together in front of you in the praying position and then turning the hands outward and pushing toward the sky as far over your head as possible will stretch the shoulders and the back. And the uncurling from the bottom up as described earlier also contributes to a more flexible back and spine.

Taking your address position with your forehead resting against a wall or post and then making your biggest turn back and your biggest turn through is another drill for flexibility. In addition you can feel what it's like to try to keep your steady head position while doing this.

Another fine drill for developing a more flexible turning move is to swing a club to the top of your backswing. Then let your right hand slide down the club shaft to the metal portion. Hold the club in your fingers of that hand and pull. The pressure on the clubshaft will cause you to stretch back further than in your regular swing.

Something you can do anywhere you are sitting is to put both feet on the floor and sit upright. Turn as far as you can to the right and back to the left. If you can grasp the back of your chair you can hold the position longer. You're simply stretching the muscles in the lower back. Chances are you can really feel these. They are usually pretty tight from holding your body upright so much of the time.

While you're sitting there you can also stretch out another set of muscles that has to work almost all the time, the neck muscles. Not only do you work those holding up the head but you also often keep a lot of stress and tension in these muscles without even knowing it. By having a daily set of stretching exercises you can help more than your golf game. Simply let your head fall forward while keeping your shoulders relaxed. You may even feel some pain between the shoulder blades but don't let the shoulders hunch up. Instead let the head go slowly down, stretching and relaxing the muscles of the upper back and neck. Then slowly let your head roll all the way to one side, to the back and to the other side. Take several seconds to do this. If you feel pain, stop and let the muscles relax naturally before continuing your circle. Do this in both directions six or eight times. Combine a big, deep breath with the forward fall of the head. Putting both hands on the head and pulling slightly forward will stretch the muscles a little further yet.

Moving off the chair and onto the floor, you can work on stretching the leg and hip muscles. Lying on your back, bend one knee and try to bring it up to your chest while pushing the lower back down toward the floor. Try to keep the other hip on the floor, too. Alternate legs and make about ten repetitions with each leg. Follow that with ten of both knees up together. This is a good stretcher for the lower back.

Sit up with the legs extended and try to lean forward to where your forehead can touch your thighs. Most of us can't get nearly to that position but try to stretch a little further each time. And don't forget to hold the position for those few seconds.

To further stretch the legs and hips get yourself into a lunge position. Have the left leg bent at the knee and the right leg extended behind you. Place both hands on the floor to help support yourself. Try to stretch low to the floor letting the right leg go further back. Change legs and repeat. Hold the position at full lunge for a few seconds. Do ten repetitions on each leg.

As I said before, there are literally hundreds of exercises you could do. Just make sure that any you attempt are done conservatively enough to prevent injury.

CHAPTER EIGHT

WARMING UP

Before leaving this concept of flexibility and stretching, I want to give you a few ideas about warming up before play. The things you choose to do at this time can either contribute to or detract from your play on those first few holes.

Ideally, you would like to have at least a half an hour to get ready to tee off when you play. Realistically that is not always possible. Ideally, you would like to be able to hit balls, chip and putt before teeing off. Again, this isn't always possible. What you can do, even when you don't have a long time or practice facilities available, is to prepare the muscles and the mind to be ready to play.

Preparing the mind means getting psyched up, becoming mentally alert. You will have studied the score card and made your overall game plan. You will look at the first hole and plan your landing area for your drive. You will have everything organized so that you aren't rushed or overly excited.

Then you need to prepare your body. Gary Wiren says that golf is the only sport he knows of in which the ''athlete'' runs from the parking lot, throws down his clubs, takes out his glove and driver, takes two swings at a cigarette butt and one at a dandelion, and says, ''I'm ready, what are we playing for?'' That's not the best way to prepare the body.

First, you need to do some basic stretching of all the parts you expect to use in the swing. That means starting with some neck rolls, coupled with deep breaths. Remember that won't hurt your anxiety control either. Then you should so some shoulder stretches. Holding your driver by both ends behind your back and stetching while turning from side to side works well for that. Putting a club behind the back underneath the elbows and turning a full shoulder and hip turn is a good positive drill for that.

Waking up the legs and feet is necessary, too. A couple of light knee bends or pulling the knees up to the chest stretches out the legs a bit.

The swing drill in which you step to the right with your left foot on the backswing and then step back left on the forward swing gets your weight moving. Circling and stetching the ankles prepares them for their work in moving the weight back and forth.

Finally, it's time to alert the hands and arms as to what you expect of them. Take two heavy clubs, a wedge and sand wedge, for example. Swing them back and forth, feeling the weight of the clubs, and allow the wrists to react to the weight. Get the arms moving and pushing the clubs away from your swing center. Stretch the swing higher and higher until you're making a three-quarter swing. The overload of the two heavy clubs will make your driver seem lighter and easy to swing.

Then immediately before getting ready to tee off take a few good swings with the club you expect to tee off with. Make them in good tempo with full turn and extension. Now your body's ready! This kind of warm-up will give you the best chance for making a playable shot off the first tee. Your only objective is to put the ball in play. You should not expect it to be the best swing of the day, but with a good warm-up and a confident plan for the shot, there's no reason it can't be. Go for it!

CHAPTER NINE

The Only Other Things You Need

Having come this far in building your golf game into the art form that you can be proud of, you must be saying to yourself, "Surely this is all I need to play this game." Well it is. Almost.

There are just two other things that I think everyone who wants to be the best golfer they can needs to know. One of those is a working knowledge of the rules of the game and the other is a working knowledge of how to use all the material found in this book, or any other book.

While they don't seem all that related at first, I think they are. They are related in that they both are in fact sets of rules. You've heard me say that the only thing really necessary for becoming a good golfer is to learn fundamentals and work hard to perfect them. That's a hard and fast rule of how to get better. Hitting the flagstick while you're putting on the green gives you a 2-stroke penalty. That's a hard and fast rule of the game.

If you want to represent yourself well at all times, both through your knowledge and through your skills, you're going to have to learn both sets of "rules."

RULES OF THE GAME

We all know that the official rules of golf are published by the United States Golf Association (USGA) and are seemingly very complex. I'm not going to waste your time quoting what you can read somewhere else. But what I am going to do is share with you some of the basic rules governing play. Those that you absolutely must know, not only to play legally and fairly, but also to help you get the best advantage allowable. And I'm going to share my ideas on those other rules of etiquette which I think are just as important to making you a good player and a good sport.

Let's look at those rules of etiquette first. Many inexperienced golfers and many others who just don't seem to care about their fellow players or the courses on which they play ignore these rules. And, yet, I know of no one who judges a player more on skill than on etiquette. Nearly every golfer can remember how it felt to be learning or playing poorly. They don't mind that. But if you show blatant disregard for others and the course, golfers DO mind that. The rules aren't so tough to remember. In fact they're pretty much common sense and courtesy. They can be grouped into four different categories for easy recall.

Be safe . . . be quick . . . be courteous . . . and be kind to the course! It's as simple as that.

Being safe means not swinging so as to endanger people. Being safe means not hitting until the group ahead is out of range, and yelling "Fore" if there's even a little danger of hitting anyone. Being safe means looking out for others' swinging around you and keeping yourself protected. Being safe means driving golf cars safely. Being safe means not throwing or beating clubs on the ground. Being safe means getting in out of lightning on the course. Being safe means not TAKING CHANCES.

Being quick means keeping up the pace of play, being ready to hit when it's your turn. Being quick means keeping your equipment with you, leaving it off the green near where you'll exit to the next hole. Being quick means planning ahead. Being quick means watching your ball until it comes to rest and sighting a landmark to help you find it. Being quick means being alert to helping others in your group look for balls. Being quick means using your time wisely, writing scores down while someone else is teeing off, not while you all are on the green. Being quick means going to your ball any time it's safe to do so. And, if everybody agrees, being quick means playing "ready golf" not waiting for the player with "honor" to tee off first.

Being courteous is just that! Treating fellow players the way you'd like to be treated. Being courteous is letting faster players play through. Being courteous is not expecting to play through if there's no place to go. Being courteous means standing quietly out of the way while others are playing. Being courteous means not blaming others for our errors. Being courteous means not stepping on a player's putting line and keeping your shadow off it. Being courteous is simply being quiet and not distracting.

Being kind to the golf course means treat it like it was yours, because it is. It's where you're playing golf. Use it; don't abuse it. Being kind to the course means taking care of the turf: replace divots, don't tear up others with practice swings or in anger; don't scrape up the greens with your spikes or your putter. Being kind to the course means leaving it like you found it. Rake traps. Pick up your litter. Don't vandalize anything. Take care of the course, because you may wish to come back and play again, and you'd like it to be even better than it was for this round.

Golf etiquette is nothing more than good manners. Good manners toward the others playing. Mother Nature and the people who look after the course. Using good etiquette is one of your most important measures as a golfer in my book. You're never too young, nor too inexperienced, nor too lacking in skill to start using it. Make sure yours is up to par.

The other rules of play you need to make sure you know can be made fairly simple too. You need to know the rules governing match play if you're playing that and those governing stroke play is that's what you're doing. What I'll do to make it simple is to list the match play ruling in every situation. Although there are some differences, many are the same.

CHAPTER NINE

One of the most sensible ways of looking at the rules of the game is to realize that the first rule of the game says you should play the ball from the tee into the hole with a stroke or series of strokes, period. Everything else is an exception to that rule. So if you try to always follow Rule 1, you'll play a simpler game by far. But as we all know, that's very seldom the case.

Let's look at a typical hole and see the rules you need to know. Teeing off — the rules say you can tee the ball between the markers and up to two club lengths behind the markers. You don't have to stand between them, only the ball needs to be there. If you tee off in front of or outside of that area, you immediately have a two-stroke penalty and you must hit again, your third shot for the hole. If you're in match play, your opponent can choose whether or not he wants you to re-tee it. Even if he makes you do it over, there is no penalty. If the ball falls off the tee, you can re-tee it with no penalty. And, of course on the tee, as everywhere else, if you make a swing at the ball and miss, it counts as a stroke.

One of the most important rules you need to know is the rule concerning out-of-bounds. If you are not properly tuned in to your aim, if you are thinking negatively, if you are aimed incorrectly, or sometimes, if you just made a bad pass at it, you may knock the ball out of bounds. O.B. is marked with white stakes or some other designated marking specific to that course (such as a roadway, fence, etc.) If you feel there is any chance that your ball is out of bounds, then you should say that you're going to play a provisional ball. That is another ball you hit immediately that you will play PROVIDING you cannot play your first one. When you come to where your first ball is lying you must determine if it is out-of-bounds. The line that determines what is out is the inside edge of the stakes. And to be out-of-bounds your entire ball must be outside that line. If any part of the ball is hanging over that inside edge onto the golf course, then you're still in bounds and in good shape. If not, then you go to your provisional ball and play it. Your score at this time will include the original stroke that hit the ball out-of-bounds, a one-stroke penalty, and the second stroke you used to hit the provisional ball. So if you were originally hitting off the tee, you are *getting ready to hit* your fourth stroke for the hole. The penalty is the same for stroke or match play.

And, actually, the penalty is the same if you were to have lost your ball. A lost ball is, by definition, any ball you can't find after five minutes of searching. If you hit a ball somewhere where there's a chance it could be lost again, it's a good idea to hit that provisional ball. Remember you don't have to count that one at all, if you haven't lost your ball or you haven't hit it out-of-bounds.

Another thing to remember about that provisional ball is that you *cannot* play it for any other reason. Suppose you find the ball you thought might be lost, but it's underneath a huge fir tree with no possible way for you to swing at it. You don't have the option to go out and play your provisional ball. You do have the option to go back to the tee and hit yet another ball and play that one but you may not play the provisional. The reason behind that seemingly strange rule is this: you are already looking at a pretty good shot sitting out there with your provisional. That might influence you to say, ''I'll just declare the first ball unplayable and go ahead and play this one.'' In effect, you'd have a choice between two balls and that's not the way the game's played. If you choose to call it an unplayable lie, and remember you are the only one who can do that for yourself and you ALWAYS have the opportunity to do that EXCEPT WHEN YOUR BALL'S IN A WATER HAZARD, you must choose one of your drop options and play from there, not from the provisional ball already sitting there.

When the ball's lost or when it's out-of-bounds you don't have a choice between two ball positions, you must play the provisional. The lost ball and O.B. ball are the only two situations that don't give you options

157

from where to hit the next shot. Each of them demands it be played from where the original shot was played, hence your penalty is both stroke and distance gained. Both are the same for match and stroke play.

Well, let's hope you've gotten off the tee of this typical hole without going O.B. or getting lost. Once the ball is in play you're not supposed to touch it with your hand or club except when executing a stroke, identifying it, or taking a drop. Playing so-called "winter rules" is certainly not condoned by the USGA, but if the circumstances demand you play them, make sure everyone knows what they are. Generally, winter rules are those that allow you to improve the lie of your ball before playing the shot. Each golf facility or group playing them has their own modifications on how this can be done. Unless so stipulated, you will be expected to play the ball as it lies.

Occasionally, a player will hit another player's ball by mistake. Because this results in a penalty for you, or for both of you if you exchange balls unknowingly, you should always look to make sure it's your ball you're getting ready to hit. In strict competition you must correct your mistake before teeing off on the next hole or you'll be disqualified. Once you determine you've played the wrong ball, you have to find the RIGHT ball. Then you go back to the spot where you think the switch was made and play the hole over. You don't have to count any of the strokes you hit with the wrong ball, but you do have to add two strokes penalty to your score for the hole. If you've done it while playing match play, you automatically lose the hole. If you've just exchanged balls, then the first one to have played the wrong ball loses the hole. If you can't decide who that was, then play continues with the wrong balls until the hole is finished. For either stroke or match play there is no penalty if you play a wrong ball out of a hazard (sand bunker or water). But you do have to go back and find your ball, or if you can't, then the ball is considered lost in a bunker or to be in the hazard in the water hazard.

Sometimes, if your ball is in heavy grass, it may be impossible for you to identify it by just looking at it. You can pick the ball up to make sure it is yours, providing you do it legally. That means you have to say you're going to do that, you have to give your playing partners the chance to come over and watch you do it, if they so desire, and once having identified it as yours, you must replace it exactly as it was. It's not legal to improve its position.

Sometimes your ball will interfere with someone else's out in the middle of the fairway. The other player can ask you to move your ball so that he can play his shot. To do this you should mark the position of your ball and then replace it after the other shot has been played.

When we were talking about the provisional ball, I mentioned an unplayable lie. That's a rule you need to know well. Basically it says that you, the player, can call your ball unplayable anywhere except in a water hazard. It doesn't apply to a water hazard because the options for play are nearly identical.

Working on a variety of recovery shots will make you less likely to need the rule. After all, it does carry a one-stroke penalty for both stroke and match play. And if you can manufacture a shot that will move the ball to a better position than one of your drop options under this rule, then you should play it. But sometimes picking up the ball and taking the penalty stroke is the smart way to play. Keep one thing in mind: Look at all your options BEFORE you pick up the ball, because your best bet may be to just leave it there and try to play it. But once you pick it up, you have to go ahead and drop it according to the rule.

The basic rule says you can move the ball any time you deem it unplayable. You have the option of dropping it anywhere within two club-lengths of where it originally was so long as you're no closer to the hole, or of taking it back to where the last shot was played, or of going on a line behind the ball keeping the place it lay between you and the flagstick.

159

CHAPTER NINE

There are several things that people get confused about with this rule. The first is that they don't really believe YOU can say it's unplayable anywhere. For example if you putt the ball down a steep green into a bunker, you could call it unplayable, take the ball back to where it was last hit from, i.e. on the green, take your one-stroke penalty and putt again. I can't say that that would be in the spirit of the rule, but it certainly would be in the letter of the rule.

Another thing that people get confused on is the third option for where you can drop the ball. Some golfers think you take the ball back along the line you hit it, going back toward the tee for example. No! That so-called "line of flight" does not exist. It's the line stretching from the flagstick through the ball's position and all the way out to the boundary of the golf course.

Jack Nicklaus caused a semi-furor on a nationally televised tournament some years ago by taking an unplayable lie in which he went back 70 or 80 yards along this line, far enough to get beyond the stand of trees he was in. He then was able to play a high approach shot over all the trees and land the ball on the green. If he had used the two-club-length option, he would have still had to recover out of the trees. Or if he had gone back to the tee, he still would not have had a chance to be on in three. He chose the option for dropping that gave him the best chance to play the next shot successfully. That's what you should do, too.

The final confusion that sometimes exists about an unplayable lie has to do with what your options are when you declare a ball unplayable in a bunker. The 1984 version of the rules makes it clear that, IF you declare your ball to be unplayable in a bunker, you can drop it within two club-lengths, BUT STILL IN THE BUNKER; you can go back along the line from the flagstick, BUT STILL IN THE BUNKER; or you can go back to the spot you played your last stroke. All of these carry the one-stroke penalty. This last option could be particularly helpful if you hit a short approach shot that barely misses the green and totally buries in the lip of the bunker. Unless you can be certain you can get out and onto the green in one, it would seem more prudent to come back and hit the approach shot over, taking your unplayable lie penalty.

Although you can't have an unplayable lie in a water hazard, the options are quite similar to those for that rule. Remember, there may be two types of water hazards on all courses. That water running across or behind the line of flight is simply called a water hazard; that running more or less parallel to it is called a lateral water hazard. Approved markings are yellow stakes or lines for water hazards and red ones for lateral hazards. If your course has no markings, then all competitors should agree which type of hazard you're playing.

Simply hitting into a water hazard carries no penalty. You're perfectly free to play the ball from it. But remember if your ball is sitting on the grass but inside the margins (the fairway edge of the stakes or lines mark the margins), you still cannot ground your club. Grounding your club, touching the surface before playing your forward swing, in either a water hazard or a sand bunker results in a two-stroke penalty in stroke play and loss of hole in match play. So long as you do not ground your club and you play the ball out of the hazard, it's no different from any other shot in the round.

But if you can't play the ball, sometimes you can't even find it because it's so far into the water, then you must take a one-stroke penalty and play from one of the drop options. Whether you find your original ball or have to drop a new one, the penalty is still only one stroke. If your ball had been in a water hazard, your options of where to drop are fewer than if it were in a lateral hazard. Basically you only have two: you can go back to the spot where you originally placed the last shot or you can go back along the line that extends from the flagstick through the spot the ball last crossed the margin of the hazard. The ball itself might have floated away from that spot but that's what you use to measure the line. Just like with an unplayable lie you can drop anywhere on that line, no closer to the hole.

If you were in a lateral hazard then you would have the same two options, going back to the original spot the ball was hit from and going back along the line from the flagstick. But you also have a couple of other places to drop: Two club-lengths from the spot where the ball last crossed the margin of the hazard OR two club-lengths from the opposite edge of the hazard, directly across from the place it last crossed the margin of the hazard. And, as usual, you can never move closer to the hole. As you can imagine that second place the other side may not always be accessible if the body of water is big. But if it were, the option would be there.

It's beginning to sound like there's nothing but trouble on this hole. But by your knowing how to use the rules to your advantage you can only add to your skills as a player. One of the things that you can't do for your advantage is to seek or give advice, unless it is from your caddie or playing partner. That means you can't ask what club I hit, but you can ask me how long the hole is. You can't ask me to club you unless we're partners, but you can use your printed yardage booklet to help yourself. In general you can ask for and give any information that is common, published knowledge. If you break this rule, it will cost you two strokes in stroke play and loss of hole in match play.

Any time during play of the hole you have the right to move loose impediments from around your ball before you play it. Loose impediments are not growing. You can't break off limbs, even dead ones. Nor can you stomp down grass and bushes to get to your ball better. Even when you move loose impediments, you must be very careful not to let your ball move. If it moves you then will have to count that movement as a stroke and add it to your score for the hole. And you must replace the ball.

But if the ball moves on the putting green while you're removing loose impediments, you will not be penalized. You still must replace it in its original position.

There are several things that can cost you one or more strokes when you are on the putting green, however. The most common mistake you can make is to hit the flagstick while you're putting from the green. Even though you're using a putter from the fringe or the fairway, you can hit the flagstick from those areas. From the green you may not. Doing so carries a two-stroke penalty in stroke play and loss of hole in match play.

Your ball hitting another player's ball also may result in a penalty for you. If you're competing in stroke play and your putt strikes another ball on the green, you will have a two-stroke penalty. You play your ball as it lies and the other person must replace his ball, even if you knocked it in the hole. In match play there is no penalty if your ball hits another player's on the green. He must replace his ball. Yours is played as it lies.

In match play there is one other difference of which you should be aware. You can concede another player's putt or concede the hole to the other player. In stroke play all players must continue putting until they have putted out.

It would be virtually impossible to cover all the rules of play that you might encounter, even in informal play. But if you learn these few basic ones and then spend a little time becoming familiar with the USGA RULES of GOLF, you'll be able to look up almost any rule you need to know. It is a game of fairness and equity. When in doubt, play it under those guidelines. When in competition, ask for a ruling from the committee. And if it's stroke play, remember you can always play what is called a ''second ball.'' That is a ball you would choose to play under the rule as you understand it while still playing your original ball under the rule as a playing partner has told you. Do not be intimidated into believing someone else, unless that individual is a rules official for the competition. Announce that you plan to play a second ball and you wish yours to count as your score, if it is ruled to be legal. That way you have both bases covered.

Being confident in knowing the rules provides one more means of confidence for yourself in playing the game. But even that won't replace soundly built skills. To perfect the fundamentals described throughout this book you will need to follow other rules as well.

RULES OF PRACTICE

Jack Nicklaus has worked as hard on his golf game as anyone I've ever known. And he's still doing so today. You may not have the time to devote yourself so completely to practice but you will still need some rules and guidelines to follow.

1. The first rule of good practice is to have a plan. So often you just go out to ''hit balls.'' That is comparable to that marksman going out to fire a few rounds. Plan some specific objective you want to meet. Practice some swing component. Work on aiming. Work on distance. Different practices will have different objectives. But always have one.

2. Practice as much as you can. Most people I have taught don't want to pay their ''sweat equity.'' Bob Toski tells of coming in crying as a child to his older brothers because his hands hurt from hitting balls. They sent him back to hit more balls. During a particularly good period of his career, Tom Watson won three tournaments in four weeks. The fourth week he wasn't entered. Instead he was working on his game with mentor Byron Nelson. He hit balls from daylight to dark three days of that week and went back to win the third one of those tournaments the next week.

If these premiere players of the game have to practice a lot, what do most amateurs need to do? Most players need to spend more time in planned practice, working toward a goal or goals and grooving their swings.

3. Practice what you don't do well. Everybody likes to hit their favorite club on the range. No one likes to hit the one they miss. Everyone likes to bang out drives. Few people will spend hours chipping and putting.

Determine what your strengths and weakness are through careful analysis of your playing rounds. Then work on the areas that are weak.

4. Take lessons. Even tour players need the analytical eye of a professional teacher to keep their games well honed. I've taken over 1,100 lessons in my life and have learned something from every one of them. Some of them confused me because the professionals used different terms or stressed different fundamentals. But I learned to be discriminating and I learned the pros I wanted to stick with. You should do the same.

5. Spend some time studying the game and the golf swing. There's not a successful player who stays that way who doesn't know a great deal about the golf swing and how they themselves swing and play. Read books. Study tips. Listen to others. And learn. Notice I didn't say anything about believing or agreeing with all of them. But evaluate them and take away what you can use.

6. Get your body and mind into the very best shape possible through practice in mental skills and training. Don't settle for less than the best from yourself in these areas. They are areas that nearly everyone can improve in without having to execute the golf swing any better. Use those advantages to help yourself.

7. Practice and play within yourself and your capabilities. Rise to the highest level possible for you. Accept your limitations of time, of talent, of technique, of physical build, of strength, of whatever you must work with. But never stop trying to improve. Never stop expecting to play better. Never stop working to lower your score. And most of all, never stop loving the game. It is like no other you will be privileged to play.

If you really want to become better these rules will be as important as those of the USGA. And just as no one likes having to take a penalty stroke, no one likes the hard work and discipline necessary to follow practice rules. But the positive results you'll see will make it all worthwhile.

CHAPTER TEN

Where We Are and How We Got Here

In any of life's activities you can can do a better job with today and tomorrow if you understand a little bit about yesterday. Trying to master your golf game is no different. Not only do you need to know about where YOU were yesterday, but it helps to understand where the game of golf was yesterday, too.

Most anyone who knows the difference between a driver and a putter knows the mystery surrounding the origins of the game. Whether it actually started in Rome with the soldiers, Holland with the Lowlanders, or Scotland with the shepherds doesn't really seem to have any effect on your learning to play better. But some of the more recent history of the game does.

After golf became a national obsession with the Scots, sometime in the 15th century, we know it began to develop rapidly into a very similar game to the one you are trying to master today. And all through that development there have been changes — evolutions if you will — in the equipment used, the course on which it is played, and even in the people who play it, which have, in turn, changed the actual golf swing and game itself. I'd like to share some of those major changes with you to help you better understand why I approach the golf swing and the game in the fundamental way I do and why I'm sure that approach will help you play better.

Even though historians tell us that the French played a game with an iron-faced club and a round (more or less), wooden ball during the 15th century, the Scotch game was played with all wooden clubs and balls

WOODEN CLUBS AND FEATHERIE BALLS *were some of the first pieces of equipment for early golfers.*

carved from boxwood. For some golfers today the equipment hasn't changed too much. Renowned musical leader the late Fred Waring had a full set of fourteen woods! For him, just as for those early players, equipment had to be specially made.

Scotch bowyers, when they weren't making bows and arrows, began to make golf clubs, mostly out of blackthorn wood. Eventually clubmakers discovered that hickory was the best wood for clubs, and that iron clubfaces could sometimes be substituted for wooden ones. And as you may know, hickory remained the staple material for club shafts until well into the 20th century!

The golf ball was changing during these centuries of evolution as well. By the 17th century golfers had rejected wooden balls and turned to a ball that would go further, the "featherie." As you can see, the one thing that seems never to have changed is the fact that golfers are always looking for new equipment to help them out! But the featherie ball, with its leather hide and feather stuffing was a real improvement. Tradition has it that the amount of feathers necessary to fill a ball was a top hat full. These were wet down, and stuffed in the cow hide which was then stitched up. When the feathers dried out the ball was very hard with the hide stretched tight.

It also shouldn't surprise you to know that about this time the frugal Scots started spending a lot of time looking for these balls when they hit them off line. Whereas the wooden balls had been fairly inexpensive, the featherie was more costly. So the powers that were had to make a rule limiting the amount of time that could be spent looking for a ball, and the rule still exists today!

The first rubber golf ball was introduced in the middle of the 19th century, the gutta-percha ball. Not only was this ball less expensive than the featherie but it also carried a longer distance. Its only drawback seemed to be that it did not necessarily fly straight. Its flight was totally unpredictable and erratic. But once it was dented and nicked up a little, it flew straighter. So, golfers, always seeking anything to help out, began to bang dents and "dimples" into their brand new balls. Modern day research in aerodynamics has proven what these early players suspected — that uneven surfaces do affect the flight of the ball. Even today ball makers are still trying to find the best pattern and right number of dimples to produce the truest and best ball flight.

The first ball to be made with uneven surfaces however didn't have dimples. Developed in 1898, the Haskell ball was the first one with a rubber center which was wound with rubber string. In addition the rubber cover had geometric lines and markings to produce greater lift and truer flight. As you can see, the golf ball by this time was beginning to resemble our modern balls. And the best thing about the Haskell ball was that there were so many of them produced that the price of a golf ball came way down.

As better clubs and balls evolved, golf courses had to be changed to continue the challenge. Those first Scottish golf "courses" were usually nothing more than publicly owned linksland. Linksland was that land formed along the estuaries of rivers where there was rich soil deposited along the sand dunes and hollows of the beach areas. And the first golf course architect was Mother Nature.

The land itself was a challenge with its scrubby gorse on the dunes, its pits of beach sand where animal burrows had caved in, and its closely grazed areas of pasture. The sea breezes provided yet another consideration for those early players. No specific holes were laid out and no maintenance program existed. Mother Nature was not only architect but golf course superintendent as well!

The Old Course at St. Andrews is generally considered to be the oldest golf course in Scotland. Records show it was in existence as early as 1414. Today it is still important, not only as the site of major events like the

1984 British Open but also because it is still a public golf course where you or I or anyone else can call for a tee time . . . even though you may have to call about a year in advance!

As golf became more popular in Scotland, actual "courses" of play evolved. Whereas originally players had just hit out, maybe to a rabbit hole agreed upon by the players themselves and then hit back in, to another hole somewhere, now they had to hit out further to keep out of each other's way. St. Andrews' design evolved in the shape of a shepherd's staff or crook. There were 12 different large putting surfaces, ten of which were used twice during a round. Because the players had to designate whether they were playing "out" to the sea or "in" to the land, golf inherited two of its modern day terms; "out" referring to the first nine holes of play and "in" to the second nine holes of play in an 18-hole round. But interestingly enough, St. Andrews started out as a 22-hole golf course, not 18.

In fact it remained a 22-hole course until sometime in the late 18th century when the Society of St. Andrews Golfers combined the first four holes into two holes which were thought to be more challenging. Since the greens were played both going out and coming in, this reduced the round to 18 holes. Even though these seem to be the facts, a lot of golfers still think those early players playing in the raw Scottish gales simply quit when the 18 jiggers of Scotch found in a bottle were all consumed!

In the early 1800's St. Andrews became The Royal and Ancient Golf Club of St. Andrews and thereby became recognized as the official home of golf. All golf courses were eventually designed with 18 holes, because St. Andrews had 18 holes. Purists thought it improper to call any place golf "links" unless it was actually built on linksland. So the term "green" was used to refer to other areas, later they were called "golfing course." Eventually this was shortened to "golf course."

But St. Andrews and Scotland weren't the only place the playing area was changing during this time. Golf had come to the new world with a golf club being founded in the United States in 1786 in Charleston, SC. In addition it had been introduced as far away as India, South Africa and Hong Kong and as nearby as England and France before the end of the 19th century. One thing had become universally obvious: golf courses were going to be different from each other, according to the geography and climate of the area.

And golf courses already in existence were changing, too. When the acceptance of the gutta-percha ball made it possible for clubmakers to use iron heads on their implements, golfers began to dig up more turf with their shots. Once the heather was dug up it often did not grow back. Instead bent grass, common to linksland, grew up in its place and fairways of shorter grass were born. Whereas there had always been limited amounts of this shorter grass, now these areas became wider.

It was about this time that the first golf course designer started actually planning golf courses rather than just letting them spring up. Allan Robertson, who was a professional at St. Andrews, is generally thought to be the first designer. At that time, you must remember, the professional was the fellow who played the best, taught others to play, made their clubs and did just about everything else at a golf links so it would seem natural he would know best how to lay out a course.

Most courses were designed by professionals or greenskeepers throughout this period. They would simply go out to a proposed area, spend a few days on site choosing natural areas for tees and greens and arrange the course around them. About the only consideration given to construction or maintenance was to make sure there would be sand available to top-dress the greens.

Not only were they busy designing new courses as the game became easier (believe it or not) with new equipment, these men often redesigned other courses to make them 18 holes. One of them, Old Tom Morris, developed a different pattern for the 18 holes. In 1891 his golf course at Muirfield, Scotland opened with two nine-hole loops, each one starting and ending at the clubhouse. This pattern, still in existence in many courses today, allows us to play only a nine-hole round when we choose.

Other changes and innovations affected courses. Specific equipment for cutting a putting hole came into use in the middle of the 19th century; metal cups were sunk into the holes in the 1870's. Irrigation of putting greens dates back to the 1880's. And the lawn mower, invented in 1830, finally made it to the golf course by the last half of that century.

But just as not all of these innovations were happening at *every* course in Scotland, not all of them were available elsewhere either. In the United States the first verified playing course for golf was a three-hole layout designed by a Scotch immigrant, John Reid in Yonkers, NY in 1888. Even though golf ''clubs'' had been established in South Carolina and Georgia in the 1700's, the members apparently had no golf courses on which to play. Only another golfer can understand the love of the game that must have made those Scotch and English settlers have a golf club with no golf course. As late as the 1980's, a golf club was formed in Juneau, Alaska, and attracted as many as 300 members, even though the closest actual golf courses were in Canada, several hundred miles away. That's real enthusiasm for the game in the tradition of the colonists.

Even though Reid and his playing buddies went ahead and expanded their course to six holes and named it the St. Andrews Golf Club, there are a number of disputes even today about where the first American course REALLY was. Courses in Pennsylvania, Vermont, Iowa, West Virginia, Florida, Illinois and even Nebraska claim to have been in existence sometime before 1888. The fact is, that no matter where it really began in this country, once it did begin, the game really spread. By 1896 there were over eighty courses open and by 1900, over NINE HUNDRED and eighty!

CHAPTER TEN

Around 1890 a Scotch professional by the name of Willie Dunn, or "Young Willie" as he was called so as not to confuse him with his father, was brought to the United States to design a golf course. This is the first record that we have of a real designer being employed. He designed and built a course way out on Long Island in New York that opened in 1891, Shinnecock Hills. Although his equipment was poor and his help was totally inexperienced in building golf courses, Willie built a course far better than any of the existing ones here in the States. That fact is borne out by the many major events still being conducted there, among them the 1986 U.S. Open.

Willie Dunn is important to us, not only because he built this fine course, but also because he went back to Scotland and told other professionals about the exciting new world of golf in America. He was convinced that the real future of the game was no longer in Scotland but in America. And because of that gospel he spread, a large number of Scotsmen moved to the United States. Some of them were professionals, some were greenskeepers, some designed courses, some were clubmakers, and some were only just interested in golf and the new world. Whatever their reasons for coming, it marked the start of something big in golf.[1]

And talking about these fellows coming over leads us to the consideration of the people who play this game. Have we evolved over the years, like the equipment and courses? I don't mean *evolved*, like the monkeys and all that stuff. But I do believe the people who play this game have changed and that also affects the way the game is played.

If you don't think people have changed, just compare the average starting line up of a professional basketball team in 1950s to one of the 1980s! Sure, the fellows today are taller. The whole population is bigger. Better food, better medical services, whatever causes it, people are bigger.

[1]Historical background from the GOLF COURSE by Geoffrey S. Cornish and Ronald E. Whitten. Used by permission.

You take a look at the doors of some of the old Scot cottages and they're barely five feet high. The Scots playing this game a hundred, or even fifty years ago were a little different than these big guys of today. Now I realize that a great many of the better tour players aren't real tall. In fact 5'10'' or 11'' seems to be pretty consistent.

Ben Hogan, Arnold Palmer, Jack Nicklaus, Tom Watson, they're all less than 6' tall. But you look back even 75 or 100 years and ninety-five out of a hundred Scotsmen would be short fellows, 5'6'' to 5'8''. Bobby Cruickshank was only about 5'2'' or so, Gene Sarazen is only 5'5'' or so. A lot of good players and a lot more of the fellows who weren't playing the professional tour but were into golf, as was a lot of the general population, were just shorter and therefore closer to the ground.

This fact alone could influence how the golf club was being swung. But there was more. Golf was played in what can only be called restrictive clothing. Even when I started playing the Tour in 1931 it was not unusual for fellows to wear dress shirts and ties. And ladies wore long, long skirts and full blouses and sweaters. It was something to swing in!

But probably the biggest factor that affected the way people swung the golf club and played the game in this country during the early part of this century was one simple thing. Most everybody taught themselves to play. After the big onslaught of Scots in the late 19th century there were many new golf courses and a lot of new players. But there weren't enough teachers and professionals who actually knew anything much about the mechanics of the game. Thousands of people learned the game and the best players got that way by working on their own game, *their* own way.

You have to remember there wasn't a lot of communication nationwide. There weren't any movies or television to show the great golfers every weekend. There were a few books maybe, but generally areas of the country were pretty self-contained. So even players who went out to play the PGA Tour often arrived with swings that were pretty unorthodox by to-

ARNOLD PALMER, *a leading player of the fifties and sixties, is just under six feet tall, as are many successful golfers.*

THIS PHOTOGRAPH *of me blasting from the sand during the 1953 PGA Championship Tournament in Detroit shows the type of clothing professionals wore.*

day's standards, but — and this is important — they worked!

The names we recognize as being excellent golfers worked in golf as professionals or clubmakers or apprenticing under some professional or clubmaker. But they had really learned to play as caddies, with other caddies. They learned by observing the players they caddied for. And even the great Bobby Jones who referred to Stewart Maiden as his teacher didn't have much instruction from him. But Hagen, Sarazen and all of them were pretty much self-taught.

The only exception in that era was Tommy Armour. He had learned to play under the British professional, George Duncan, before coming over here. He told me himself that he had over 900 lessons from different English professionals before coming to the United States as an amateur in the twenties. But Armour was an exception in many ways. He was also taller than some of the other fellows playing around that time. And he played the ball from a little different position because of his lack of sight in one eye.

Harry Vardon, who was the great British player most often known as the "inventor" of the Vardon grip, had the opportunity to become known as a teacher. In 1898 the Spalding manufacturing company contracted with Vardon to endorse their new golf ball, one of the last of the gutta-percha balls. It was called the Vardon Flyer. And around 1900 Spalding sent Vardon around the whole country promoting the Vardon Flyer and the clubs he endorsed, the Vardon Autographs.

To the best of my knowledge this was the first time any athlete had been asked to endorse equipment. With all the different forms of mass communication today it doesn't seem so strange but it certainly was a new twist back then. Because there wasn't any professional association or organized tour at that time, both professional and amateur players were featured in magazine articles, paintings and so forth. Up through the 1920s this was pretty common practice. Probably the great Bobby Jones, who still holds the best record in amateur golf, was the last highly honored amateur.

TOMMY ARMOUR *had the advantage of professional lessons early in his career as a golfer.*

HARRY VARDON *is known not only for the grip bearing his name, but also as the first athlete paid to endorse equipment.*

BOBBY JONES *is still recognized as the greatest amateur competitor the United States has produced.*

CHAPTER TEN

So given the background that, first, there weren't many teachers and second, those there were came from the British Isles, it isn't surprising to learn that even when players' swings began to look more alike they didn't look exactly like the tour player's swing today.

A golf swing mastered by a short player in a starched shirt, tie and even suit coat, sometimes playing on a wind-swept links course with hard fairways and small greens, looked a little bit different. Harry Vardon himself even had a collapsed, or significantly bent left arm at the top of his back-swing. And because so many of them were shorter, the swing looked flatter.

The swing of the twenties and thirties used the hands a lot more. Why? Because most players still used hickory shafted clubs. The USGA had approved steel shafts in 1925 but a lot of companies still offered clubs in either steel or hickory shafts throughout the 1930s. In fact Johnny Fischer won the Amateur in 1936 still using hickory shafts.

Hickory shafted clubs tended to turn and torque more during the swing than the steel shafts of today's clubs. Feel and timing were terrifically important in using these clubs. A lot of players liked to make sure they used the same one or two clubmakers so they would have an idea of how that man's clubs would respond. You have to remember that the club-maker actually sanded and planed the shafts until he got them the way he wanted them. And not only did these shafts just torque, they warped, bent and even broke quite often. I remember talking to MacDonald (Mac) Smith once. He was one of the greatest hitters of the ball of that era himself but he also had a pro job up in New York State somewhere. At that time he had four Scotsmen working full time for him doing nothing but mak-ing hickory shafts and re-shafting clubs, a service that he said cost him about $1000 a week in salaries!

Because this idea of feel was so important and because the wrists had to be free for greater movement, the grip on the club was different back then too. The club was held a bit more up into the fingers of the left hand

"MAC" SMITH was one of many club professionals who played competitive golf on "the tour" during his off-season.

CRAIG WOOD, *a great professional player in his own right, was one of my contemporaries playing the tour in the thirties.*

and both hands were turned more over to the right than many of today's players' grips. So at the top of the backswing you would see more of a bend at the wrist of the left hand, what you would call a cupped position.

Another real difference between the players' swings back then and what we see now is the set-up. The Scottish and British influences was seen in the fact the players back then set up so as to curve the ball from right to left. That is, they aimed out to the right, often with either a closed or open stance and played the ball low and hooking to keep it below the high winds found on almost all links courses. Another reason for that low rolling ball was that the fairways were not routinely irrigated the way they are now so you could get a lot of extra yardage from the roll.

Craig Wood, himself a great player who was tied in the 1935 Masters by Gene Sarazen on that fateful day Sarazen had a double eagle on #15, told me a story about playing at Winged Foot with Bobby Jones. They were playing sometime after Jones had won the Open there in 1929. Between the Open and the round they were playing, Winged Foot had started to water fairways. Jones remarked to Wood that he had lost over *fifty yards* on his drives because of the loss of the roll on the fairway.

The look of the swing was different back then, too. Whereas you see the players of today take the club back on the target line and into a fairly upright position, players like Jones, Hagen, Sarazen and so on took the club more quickly inside the target line and swung it up and around more, not so much up over the shoulder. Since the heel came pretty far off the ground and the club was often dragged back with the hands in a long sweeping swing, the players looked like they were swinging flatter. And because the downswing and follow-through had more of an early hip turn and less leg drive, they looked like they sort of slapped the club through the ball.

The fact of the matter is though, that then as now, fundamental basic skills produced a repeatable efficient position at the moment of truth . . .

WALTER HAGAN, *known as "the Haig," typified the classical swing.*

when the clubhead meets the ball. Any golfer of any era who was or is successful has had that same good position at impact. Hands leading clubhead. Clubface square to target. Swing accelerating through the ball. Head behind the ball.

And the second fact of the matter is that, then as now, knowing what to do and then spending the time in practice to master it is the secret to becoming a good player. The game hasn't changed as much as we think it has. Sure, there have been some changes, but even colored balls go back to Wilson's 1928 Hol-Hi and Dura-Dist balls, both available in canary or oriole for only $10.75 per dozen! Equipment gets better but it's still people, not machines swinging the clubs and hitting the balls. The golf courses have improved tremendously. The superintendents of today do a fantastic job in keeping courses both beautiful and playable. But the thing that has really changed is that now everyone who swings a golf club can KNOW what to do. That doesn't mean that everyone can do it, understand.

But through research and mass communication everyone can learn the basic fundamentals that go into making a sound, efficient golf swing. The fundamentals you will learn about in this book are the very same ones that Jack Nicklaus learned from me starting when he was ten years old. And they are the ones that took him to where he is today, still possessing the best record of any professional golfer, past or present.

Sure, talent makes a difference. That's what the Good Lord gives us. But technique, now that's what we can learn. And technique can make up for a lack of talent. Sam Snead has talent galore, adding a little bit of technique made him a great golfer. Ben Hogan needed more technique but he too is one of the greatest golfers who ever swung a stick.

You may have a lot of talent or a little, but by mastering the fundamentals of a sound swing, you can surely improve your play. And no matter if you're short or tall, young or old, you can see players on televi-

JACK NICKLAUS, *fourth from left, getting an early lesson at my club in Ohio.*

sion and on videotapes who fit your body type and age category. You will still see individual differences, but not so many as existed 50 or 60 years ago.

Research in areas like biomechanics and motor learning has established principles and models of the most efficient swing patterns. Professional organizations like the PGA and LPGA have trained professionals how to teach golfers these patterns. And every one of them addresses the same fundamentals that we have been talking about in this book.

There are no gimmicks in learning the golf swing. My personal feeling is that it takes a minimum of five years to learn to play this game. When I started teaching young Mr. Nicklaus he was ten. At 15 he won his first event. Learning to ''play'' golf is like learning to play the piano, you've got to practice a lot of scales before mastering a symphony.

In this book I've tried to give you numerous ''scales'' to practice, some are simple, some are more complex. I have been honest with you about how much practice you will need. But if you love this game as I do, your work will be a labor of love.

As Dinah Shore described it, ''It is that frustrating lover who is never there when you need him, lets you down when you count on him, and seems to be only one disappointment after another. But on the those occasions when he does come around, he is so thoroughly satisfying that everything else is forgiven and forgotten!'' Golf is exactly that lover for millions of us. It will never be predictable because human beings are not predictable. It will never be boring because the challenge is not static. The challenge is alive and changing. The challenge of the game of golf is not the course or the swing. It is yourself, my friend. It has always been so. It will always be so.

INDEX